Quantum Negotiation

Karen S. Walch | Stephan M. Mardyks | Joerg Schmitz

Quantum Negotiation

The Art of Getting What You Need

WILEY

Published by John Wiley & Sons, Inc., Hoboken, New Jersey
Published simultaneously in Canada

For general information about our other products and services, please contact our Customer Care Department within the United States at (800) 762-2974, outside the United States at (317) 572-3993 or fax (317) 572-4002.

Wiley publishes in a variety of print and electronic formats and by print-on-demand. Some material included with standard print versions of this book may not be included in e-books or in print-on-demand. If this book refers to media such as a CD or DVD that is not included in the version you purchased, you may download this material at http://booksupport.wiley.com. For more information about Wiley products, visit www.wiley.com.

Library of Congress Cataloging-in-Publication Data is Available:

ISBN 9781119374862 (Hardcover)
ISBN 9781119374909 (ePDF)
ISBN 9781119374879 (ePub)

Cover Design: Wiley
Cover Image: © aleksandarvelasevic/iStockphoto

Printed in the United States of America

10 9 8 7 6 5 4 3 2 1

Contents

Acknowledgments

We would like to thank our spouses, Paul, Marie-Genet, and Latha, and our families for their support, patience, and enthusiasm for this project.

Our sincere gratitude goes to our dedicated team who played an instrumental role in guiding this book to publication:

- David M. R. Covey, for his invaluable contributions to *Quantum Negotiation* and ongoing support
- Christina Schmitz, David Westley Covey, Jacob Covey, Liz Gotter, and Scott Henderson, who were instrumental in helping us organize our thoughts
- The team at Wiley for their ongoing support and for patiently guiding this book to publication
- All our Quantum Negotiation partners and colleagues across the world

We also would like to thank our clients worldwide and the many negotiators we have met along the way who have told us their stories and placed their trust and confidence in us.

Finally, we dedicate this book to all the leaders, managers, entrepreneurs, professionals, and negotiation experts who are on a journey of true value creation.

We wish you the success you truly deserve.

The Authors

Karen S. Walch, PhD, is a partner at Clair-Buoyant™ Leadership, LLC, and co-creator of the Quantum Negotiation Certification programs. She is an Emeritus faculty member of Thunderbird School of Global Management. Karen specializes in the social interaction skills of negotiation, collaboration, influence, and inclusion. Her facilitation and coaching are focused on developing leadership behaviors for maximum personal and organizational impact in a dynamic and disruptive global economy.

Stephan M. Mardyks is a world-renowned expert in the field of global learning and development. He has conducted countless strategic negotiations in over one hundred countries. Stephan is the founder of Wisdom Destinations, the co-CEO of SMCOV, and cofounder of TrapTales and Streamline Certified. He is also managing partner at Lead in English and ThomasLeland. His past experiences include serving as Co-COO at FranklinCovey. Stephan is the coauthor of *Trap Tales*, *Leading in English*, and *Said & Done*.

 **Joerg Schmitz** is cofounder and managing partner at ThomasLeland. He is a business anthropologist with extensive experience helping leaders and organizations navigate the challenges and opportunities of culture and globalization. As a senior advisor and consultant, he has developed innovative approaches to intercultural management, diversity and inclusiveness, global talent and team optimization, and leadership development. Joerg is the coauthor of *Leading in English*.

For more information about Quantum Negotiation, please visit the website at www.quantumnegotiation.com

Foreword

More than thirty years ago David Lax and James Sebenius coined the term "the negotiator's dilemma" in their classic book, *The Manager as Negotiator.* It's the so-called tension between creating value (expanding the proverbial pie) and claiming it (capturing a favorable slice of it).

The tension derives from two opposing impulses. Value creation requires recognition of the parties' respective interests. If they bluff and bluster in order to mask their true priorities, they'll be unable to see how to generate mutual gains by trading creatively on their differing priorities. On the other hand, if one negotiator unilaterally reveals his or her interests while the other does not, the former risks being exploited. The pie may be expanded, but the sly party will get the lion's share.

The creating-claiming tension (cooperating and competing, if you prefer) isn't merely about outcomes, though. It is more fundamentally about values, identity, and relationships—specifically, self-regard versus concern for others. Two thousand years ago Hillel posed two questions that are inherent in negotiations today. "If I am not for myself," Hillel asked, "then who will be for me? But if I am only for myself, what am I?"

Identifying dilemmas, be they substantive or moral, is one thing. Managing them effectively is quite another. Most negotiation books skirt this territory. Yes, some writers address the ethics of specific tactics (such as lying), though typically without exploring foundational principles, attitudes, and beliefs. Now at last, the arrival of *Quantum Negotiation* warmly invites readers to reflect more deeply about the social nature of a process that is essential in both our professional and our personal lives.

The authors' much-needed framework builds on and integrates five key insights. First, unlike many writers who take an individualistic approach, their unit of analysis is the interaction between the parties. And so it must be. Negotiation is inherently a social activity. Each party brings his or her attitudes (conscious and otherwise) about what the specific transaction encompasses and, more broadly, what negotiation itself entails. In short, the authors here focus on the dance rather than the steps of a single dancer.

That perspective yields a second insight, namely that negotiation is necessarily a dynamic process. I am not speaking narrowly of the back-and-forth exchange of offers and demands. Rather I'm commending the authors' emphasis on how the process itself is always cocreated, especially in regard to the way that relationships emerge. Will the parties be friends or foes, for example? And what are the tacit rules of engagement? Will this be easy or will it be hard? Such questions never can be answered unilaterally. They must be jointly determined. Exactly how things will play out—even between people who know each other well—is seldom fully certain.

The authors take those first two points and add a third, by emphasizing the physical and emotional ways that we experience negotiation. They introduce us to two archetypes who pose questions to the authors throughout the book. First there's Wendy, who relishes negotiation and the thrill of besting her counterparts. And then there's Thomas, for whom the mere thought of the process triggers dread and self-doubt. It's not the intent of these authors, however, to pigeonhole people or to tell readers to suppress their emotions. Quite the opposite, in fact. Rather, they show how self-awareness and empathy can be the basis of more satisfying results for all concerned.

They link this third insight to a fourth by reminding us how loaded are some of the terms we commonly use, most notably the word "negotiation" itself. For many people it calls up associations about power, status, vulnerability, and competence.

The word also implies some sort of conditional trading, as in "I'll give you some of this, if you give me some of that." That framing brings with it an economic outlook, often at the expense of other considerations. To be sure, tangible concerns matter. A candidate for a new job will need to earn enough money to pay her rent, but she'll also want the resources and guidance to perform well. In addition, she'll care about respect and fairness.

How we name things shapes our perceptions and drives our behavior. Saying that we are "negotiating pay" takes us down one path. Seeing ourselves as "developing a job description" takes us down another.

Weaving together these first four insights (interaction, dynamics, embodied experience, and a fresh look at framing) the authors build a compelling case for the importance of the mindset that we bring to the process. Here the authors coach Wendy and Thomas to adopt a broader, socio-centric view of negotiation, one that prompts each to see how his or her particular sense of self is expressed and enacted through dealings with others. The authors also remind us of how, in this day and age, negotiation and leadership are closely intertwined, as each requires openhearted engagement. In addition, the authors provide a practical Quantum Negotiation planning framework.

Most of us know some people like Wendy, as well as others who are closer to Thomas in temperament. In quiet moments, at different times, we may have heard whispers of each of them in our own minds. The question then is whom do we want to summon when we are negotiating for ourselves or leading others? As for myself, I cannot imagine a better companion and guide than a nimble, buoyant, and empathetic Quantum Negotiator.

Introduction: What Comes to Mind When You Think of Negotiation?

We tend to get two distinct reactions to this question.

Some people pride themselves as being savvy dealmakers, and are excited by the idea of negotiation. They love to tell us about their most memorable negotiation, reporting with pride how they achieved a particularly desirable outcome through some savvy maneuver.

For others, the mere topic triggers doubt about their own abilities and sense of self, eroding confidence in otherwise very confident people. They confess that they dread negotiations and easily feel taken advantage of. They do not see themselves as shrewd enough or assertive enough, and so they prefer to avoid negotiation wherever possible.

Both of these reactions stem from a conventional view of negotiation as a battlefield, in which the negotiator with superior strategy and tactics will prevail. If you don't know the tactics and countertactics, or if you're not willing to play the game, you don't stand a chance against your opponent. The outcome of such negotiations is deeply tied into our sense of self—after it is over, you are either the heroic winner or the weakling who got taken advantage of.

Although the idea of "win-win" may be regarded as the common aspiration, it is not how most people experience negotiations or choose to behave when negotiating. In reality, negotiation behaviors follow an "I win more, you win less" approach, matched by high levels of distrust and a struggle over power and control.

We'd like to offer you a better approach.

We'd like to offer you an approach that allows the savvy dealmaker to obtain even *more* value from their negotiations, and gives self-doubters the confidence to get what they need without having to accommodate.

We invite you to set aside the conventional approach toward negotiation for a moment and look at the topic through a new lens. The conventional view is not serving you.

Paula's Story

Paula, an ambitious sales rep for an innovative shoe manufacturer, has been negotiating with a large wholesale retailer, a "Goliath" in the industry. From her perspective, the retailer—more precisely, Ben, their buyer— "wasn't interested in playing fair." Ben continually reminded her of the retailer's single-minded and presumably nonnegotiable mantra of low prices.

Paula needed this deal and knew that Ben needed it too. Her shoes were in high demand—the shoe manufacturer had grown explosively through the endorsements of popular fashion bloggers who loved the unique design and interchangeable components. A line of shoe accessories was about to launch in a few months and the demand was incredible, particularly among teenage girls. The company had big growth plans to expand into new markets.

A partnership with "Goliath" could solve the challenge to meet the explosive demand. Paula also needed this win to accelerate her career. She knew that failure to negotiate this relationship would damage her company and, as a result, her career opportunities within it.

Driven to win, Paula took an aggressive negotiation stance. She started with a tough low-ball opening price position and referred often to Joe, her VP of Sales, as the intransigent "bad cop." As Ben showed no interest in a long-term relationship, she pushed on a settlement price close to her offer price, aggressively dismissing Ben's assertions.

She applied numerous tricks she had picked up from books on negotiation and from her mentors. She was keenly aware of the hurdles women faced in negotiations with men like Ben, who was well advanced in his career and smug in his belief that all the leverage was with his "Goliath." She wasn't about to let him walk all over her.

Paula also had some cards up her sleeve. Significant time and planning went into a high-stakes gamble early in the negotiation, namely to bluff on a threat to expose Ben's company's discriminatory labor practices. She also aggressively overwhelmed Ben with thousands of pages of documentation about what he called the "feeble" retailer competition.

Now, however, after three months of a controlled, "smart" strategy and tactics, she was at an impasse. Ben and Paula ended their last two-hour meeting in anger and frustration. With still no agreement and a lot of bad feelings all around, the clock was ticking toward the demise of what could be the most important deal of her life.

Paula stands in for the hundreds of negotiators we have met who have exhausted the conventional negotiation approach. This approach has been glorified in a list of tactics and countertactics and an underlying set of assumptions that are poorly aligned with a professed "win-win" approach.

Even with a tremendous body of negotiation advice, and an abundant offering of negotiation seminars, negotiators can find success to be elusive, despite their best attempts to put the current wisdom into practice.

The pressure and aspiration to succeed may lead to a negotiation stance that amounts to what is essentially a high-stakes gamble, with no assured outcome. The resulting stalemate benefits neither party and leads to nerve-wracking drama that decreases the probability of success and alienates the negotiating parties from each other and their mutually beneficial opportunities.

At the same time, "designated negotiators" find that the set of hard-nosed strategies and tactics, presumed to be the essence of negotiation success, undermine deeply held values, attitudes, and intentions. Hardball strategies, in addition to their underlying belief system and assumptions, may contradict negotiators' sense of self and aspirations for authentic, positive relationships. The resulting intrapersonal and interpersonal conflict can alienate negotiators as much from others as from themselves, induce insecurity, and may jeopardize their true potential and satisfaction.

Martin's Story

Martin was nominated to negotiate a $4 million reduction in the purchase price of a platform acquisition after discovering misplaced reporting codes in the company's financial statements. His company, MCC, is a private equity firm seeking to buy WINSOME, a consumer electronics distributor operating across thirteen countries. WINSOME's rep, Renaldo, was assigned to negotiate with Martin. WINSOME had no CEO or CFO because it had gone through several restructurings in the past few years, resulting in misaligned financial reporting systems. To complicate things further, WINSOME had never been separately audited.

As an accountant, Martin did not feel like a negotiator. He was doubtful of his ability to go up against Renaldo, a professional negotiator. Martin knew that there had been little oversight at WINSOME and he had discovered inconsistencies in their reporting. However, he was intimidated with how firm and argumentative Renaldo was in their interactions. Martin found himself foregoing his own concerns, and felt vulnerable to Renaldo's competitive and dismissive attitude.

While being cooperative and accommodating to Renaldo's situation, Martin behaved in a generous way, yielding to Renaldo's strong point of view. He did not like the tension in their conversations, and didn't want to come off as pushy or inconsiderate. By being unassertive and trying to develop a good relationship with Renaldo, Martin avoided unpleasant topics.

That didn't change the fact that Martin ultimately needed Renaldo to cooperate with him if Martin was to take leadership of the new acquisition's financial system. After several months of negotiating, Martin had to report to his board that he still had not gotten the price reduction they had asked him to negotiate. As he left the meeting, Martin felt this was the end of his much-desired new leadership opportunity. His sense of failure and disappointment in himself reinforced his belief that he was simply not a good negotiator.

For nonprofessional negotiators, the very term "negotiation" can induce mild to strong levels of anxiety and insecurity. More than almost any other type of human interaction, negotiation is associated with high stakes, risk, distrust, and unpredictability. Perhaps this is what the volumes of literature and seminars take advantage of. They fill the need for the assurance and certainty that we seek. Defaulting to strategies and tactics that are often highly manipulative, and sometimes downright deceptive, only panders to this insecurity.

The contention at the heart of this book is that success in negotiation does not stem from such strategies and tactics at all.

A Quantum Perspective

Over years of working with negotiators, we have observed that lasting success is connected to attentiveness to small, seemingly insignificant aspects of their relationships.

We find parallels in the world of physics. For many years, Newtonian physics held that atoms are separate and can be controlled in a linear, command-control, predictable way. In the same way, traditional negotiation theory argued that negotiators are separate and would find most success with efficient, fear-based, reward-punishment strategies.

However, quantum science discovered that below Newtonian matter lies an interconnected web of subparticles known as quanta. Previously unseen, these quanta represent a multidimensional, unifying, unseen energy that forms the basis of our physical reality.

Similarly, we contend that negotiators are not separate and isolated from one another; they are part of one interdependent whole of a relationship, team, or organization. In fact, the very act of negotiation affirms the inherent interconnectedness and interdependence.

This concept has provided profound insights about how to get more of what you need in life. The difference comes in making the choice to be conscious of the emotional, neurological, and strategic interconnectedness of social life, and then manifesting that consciousness by how we show up with those that we seek to influence. From this perspective, negotiation does not have to be intimidating or anxiety inducing, because it is the deliberate practice of interdependence. We have observed a small group of leaders and negotiators who rely on this practice and have been astounded by their success as they have identified the common misconceptions surrounding negotiation, and have made changes to their lives to better get what they need.

In his book, *The Speed of Trust*, Stephen M. R. Covey's account of Warren Buffett's negotiation to acquire McLane Distribution from Walmart is a highly visible example not only of the "speed of trust," but also of Quantum Negotiation. A deal of this magnitude would minimally take several months to complete. But because both parties were attuned to each other and shared a sense of mutuality, the usual hurdles and complications were not just reduced, but circumvented altogether. As Buffett wrote in his annual report: "We did no 'due diligence.'"

Rather than focusing on the goal of surviving as an independent winner, Quantum Negotiators can embrace the uncertainty and anxiety in their human nervous system by remembering how unified they are at the quantum level. They have more success, satisfaction, and energy in meeting their needs, getting support, and enjoying life's resources. As a result, they create sustainable and resilient outcomes.

Quantum Negotiation presents a more inclusive paradigm as an alternative to the conventional practice, which often amounts to little more than Machiavellian behavior disguised by the language of win–win. Illuminating the quantum reality of negotiation and illustrating its practice gives every negotiator a fundamental choice of consciousness.

Making this choice in favor of a quantum approach seems even more relevant when we consider that leaders and negotiators increasingly cope in an ocean of complexity, uncertainty, turbulence, disruption, and cultural shifts. Particularly under such disruptive and accelerated VUCA conditions (volatile, uncertain, complex, and ambiguous) we find the distinction between leading and negotiating to be blurry at best.

Informal Negotiation

Negotiation, particularly in its Western conceptions, is associated with the explicit pursuit of contractual outcomes or agreements. (We call it Negotiation with "the big N.") We tend to think of "a negotiation" as something taking place in a boardroom, or at a car dealership.

However, we are negotiating much more frequently than we often realize. In fact, we are negotiating any time there is something that we need, and we must work through someone else to get it. Whenever we calibrate expectations, create new ways of doing things, share limited budget resources at home and work, or cooperate to solve pressing problems, we are negotiating. We are practicing the art of getting what we need by engaging with others.

It is helpful, therefore, to cast our understanding of negotiation widely and to think more deeply about our skill and identity as negotiators. Indeed, these are the defining characteristics of "Quantum Negotiators" and "Quantum Leaders." To a degree, both terms are interchangeable, as negotiations, both formal and informal, are the arena for leadership.

Successful leadership is contingent on the negotiation of agreements about perceptions and behavior. The process of negotiating and the resultant agreements behind these "micronegotiations" are more tacit and implicit, and require a continual dialogue that allows contributors to offer their best in an increasingly collaborative team- and project-based work environment. We call this negotiation with "the little n."

Lina's Story

Lina Jessen was asked to manage a project to develop new values for a multinational organization headquartered in the Nordics, with key operations in Finland, Sweden, Denmark, Norway, the United Kingdom, Central Europe, and the United States. The CEO was committed to transforming the company to a purpose-driven and values-led organization. The existing values statement had become well entrenched, and although it was neither inspiring nor aspirational, particularly to a younger generation that was difficult to attract and retain, it served the company well.

The organization was extremely fragmented and siloed into proud and independent business units and local operations. Headquarter-driven changes were routinely met with strong resistance, both overt and covert. This tendency was strongest in the US operations, where the existing values statement had been developed. The culture there was such that defiance of the headquarter mandates was an open act of heroism and a badge of honor, celebrated among local leaders. The seeming futility of Lina's mission was underscored to her after she gave a brief introductory presentation about her project. An influential leader approached her after the presentation and commented that she might as well give up as there was "no chance in hell" that the organization would move away from its current values.

Lina was only too aware of this prevalent attitude from a one-year rotation in the United States a few years prior. In addition, being a project manager gave her almost no leverage with local leaders. She was distraught and discouraged, and the project had not even fully kicked-off yet.

Lina may not see herself as a negotiator in the classic sense of needing to gain a formal, contractual agreement. But her mission, in fact, resembled the most complex and delicate of international negotiations. She needed to navigate corporate politics and power dynamics in the pursuit of credible support for an intangible—a new set of values. She had very little real leverage, which made this a daunting task to be sure.

Lina stands in for anyone in a complex, highly matrixed, and geographically dispersed organization where their success is dependent on the ability to influence and negotiate. When this type of leadership takes place in highly unfavorable conditions, such as when benefits are not readily apparent to one's counterpart and it is easy to be dismissed, ignored, or sidelined, leadership and negotiation are just two sides of the same coin. For that very reason, we are using the terms leader and negotiator interchangeably in this book.

Leadership and negotiation are both centrally focused on an intricate social process that includes converging the interests of multiple stakeholders, creating explicit or implicit agreements, aligning expectations and understanding, and shaping choices and behaviors in accordance with expectations and understanding. The quantum approach to negotiation and leadership that we advance in this publication makes this intricate social process, and our part in it, the central focus.

With orientation and attentiveness to the invisible forces of social interaction, we find that negotiators are able to be buoyant and adaptable in their style. As an observer of one's own and others' emotional, social, physical, and spiritual needs, Quantum Leaders are able to be clear and anchored about their own needs. This anchoring serves as a foundation for buoyant behavior when adapting to uncertain environments and diverse viewpoints.

We have found this perspective missing or underrepresented in many of the current approaches to negotiations, which is why we decided to add our unique take on negotiation that will be a companion on your own journey to becoming a Quantum Negotiator and Leader.

The Quantum Approach

We have been developing this approach for a few years now, but we are publishing it, coincidentally, at a time when its central themes, practices, and reflections are more important than ever. This book arrives against the backdrop of the rise in increasingly polarized public and social discourse.

Our core contention is that people involved in leading or negotiating—whether in pursuit of classic contractual outcomes ("the big N") or as part of the continual dialogue that allows contributors to offer their best ("the little n")—are best served by adopting a sociocentric, interdependent mindset.

This mindset is highly relevant to two of the more compelling trends of our times. We reject the recent repopularization of egocentric, winner-versus-loser styles captured by the return of triumphalism, brinksmanship, and the disregard for cooperation and compromise that so typifies much of our public discourse. We also believe that a more interconnected world, with the ability to harness the potential creativity of billions of new members of the global economy, will require inclusive, collaborative leaders and negotiators fully engaged in creating conditions where people can deliver their best. Our understanding of success needs to be guided by these criteria and conditions.

Mary Parker Follett coined the term "power with" rather than "power over" others in negotiation. Quantum Negotiators have explored this first approach versus the coercive "power over" approach when leading others. Quantum Negotiators use a set of negotiation rules, customs, and preparation techniques that produce more sustainable, prosperous, and satisfying agreements for today.

Quantum Negotiation is concerned with developing the mindset and skills required to attain the most satisfactory outcomes, in the hopes of creating a future work and social environment that focuses on elevating everyone's participation and assists people in developing to their fullest potential. We address the reality of seductive hardball and coercive negotiation practices, but we focus on how to engage the human spirit and its power to create new opportunities and resources.

This book features how Quantum Negotiators address the life and work skills of getting what they need when engaging with others. Although it may not seem that Paula, Martin, and Lina fit our description, none of them is aware yet of the journey they are on to become Quantum Negotiators. You will meet them again in the final chapter and understand the powerful transformative impact a Quantum approach has made. They have learned that negotiating is about more than contracts; it's also at the very core of navigating life and leading others. We succeed and thrive most when working with, rather than against others.

Accommodating Negotiation— No Power	Coercive Negotiation— Power Over	Quantum Negotiation— Power With
Worry that your counterpart will take advantage of you	Exploit your counterpart	Create value together with your counterpart
Wishes they knew more tactics and worries what their counterpart will do	Study vulnerabilities and manipulation tactics to get an edge	Study yourself and your counterpart to find more potential sources of value
Will sacrifice my win to avoid making our relationship uncomfortable	Let's find a win-win, but where I win more and you win less	Let's explore how we can both win as much as possible
Does not know the process of a negotiation and defers to their counterpart to take charge	Takes charge early and tries to maintain control	Make yourself vulnerable and heard and encourage your counterpart to do the same
Asks subordinates to do their work but makes up for where they slack off	"Knows best" and requires subordinates to work his or her way	Creates an environment for subordinates to develop and give their best
No power	"Power over"	"Power with"
Dependent	Independent	Interdependent
Give in	Dominate	Influence
Capitulation	Gamesmanship	Style-shifting
Martyrdom	Coercion	Mutual understanding
Doesn't see	Plans for the seen	Explores both the seen and unseen
Avoidance of negotiation	20th century negotiation	21st century negotiation

©2015 Quantum Negotiation

About This Book

To support the journey of discovery, reflection, and action that we hope to inspire, we have structured this book in three parts. You will meet Wendy, who sees negotiation as a battle of wills, and Thomas, who doubts his negotiation ability and tends to be very anxious when getting what he needs from others. They will ask questions, like you the reader may be thinking, about some of the themes in each chapter.

Part I takes us through a sequence of three fundamental assumptions about negotiations and our perception of ourselves, our counterparts, and the overall relationship. This acquaints us with the key elements of the Quantum Negotiation (QN) preparation model.

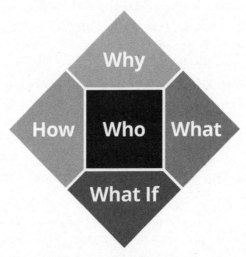

©2015 Quantum Negotiation

Chapter 1 (The WHO & WHY of Quantum Negotiation) explores who we are as negotiators in the context of our social conditioning. Our human dimensions in the cognitive, psychological, social, physical, and spiritual fields receive central attention. This is a key point of departure, as Quantum Negotiators have a strong sense of self and identity, and are anchored to their own experiences. In addition, they have the curiosity, the resilience, and the intelligence to understand another's point of view and interests.

We focus on "WHO" we are and "WHY" we need to meet those needs in an agreement with our counterpart. We invite you to reflect and prepare on all human dimensions and to consider the same exploration for a counterpart or those who need to follow.

Chapter 2 (The WHAT & WHAT IF of Quantum Negotiation) recognizes that while most often may stop our preparation with the focus on self, it really is only the foundational step for Quantum Negotiators. Quantum Negotiators operate with a broader sense of awareness, assumptions, and skills. They also shift their focus to the other and to understand more clearly what their counterpart wants in a negotiation. In addition, Quantum Negotiators explore the quality of the relationship involved. This chapter explores more of the Quantum Negotiation preparation model by discovering "WHAT" we want as negotiators and why we want it.

In addition, this chapter will explore the "WHAT IF" dimension of the QN model and look at the alternatives from both our own and our counterpart's perspective. In preparation, Quantum Negotiators think about what their alternatives—and their counterpart's alternatives—might be if they cannot reach an agreement.

Chapter 3 (The HOW of Quantum Negotiation) applies key findings about emotional and social intelligence, which suggest that negotiators can increase the power to influence not for manipulation, but for more productive facilitation practices. Increasingly, Quantum Leaders require vital facilitation skills that foster sustainable agreements that meet not only their own objectives, but that also assist others in accomplishing their own. Quantum Leaders have a facilitation talent that is accomplished by what social neuroscientists say is "leveraging the system of brain interconnectedness and coordination of left and right brain hemispheres." When interpersonal competencies are built on specific neural circuits and related endocrine systems, negotiators increase their effectiveness to cooperate and be more inclusive of others.

A Quantum Negotiator mindfully responds to others and the relationship rather than reacting to primal stress. This chapter explores reframing in the context of relationships and "HOW" we want to behave as Quantum Negotiators. We conclude this chapter with a focus on "HOW" we get what we want when negotiating with others. Quantum Negotiators are flexible in their behavior, while being anchored in their own values.

Part II is something of an interlude before diving deeper into the underlying assumptions of our belief structure. This interlude provides a series of Quantum Negotiation tools for preparation and a reference checklist for Quantum Negotiation behaviors. The tools in this section will help clarify not only what we want in a negotiation, but also why we need it, and how to explore the same for counterparts and stakeholders. This material is designed to help apply the ideas from Part I.

Engaged application, however, will surface profound challenges and questions that reach deep into our worldview. Chapters 4, 5, and 6 make up **Part III**.

Chapter 4 (Independence Is a Powerful Illusion) explores basic assumptions related to agency and motivation that stem from a glorification of independence. From physics to social psychology and neuroscience, there is evidence that we live in an incredibly interconnected world. We address why we need to master the art of interdependence as we negotiate expectations. Quantum Negotiators understand the reality of interdependence and the ways to create and measure the impact of social capital.

In addition to assessing the tangible outcomes in a negotiation, such as the value of the deal, or resources benefited, Quantum Negotiators can assess their intangible social capital. The trustworthiness of their networks and relationships increases the collaboration, support, and sharing others provide to them. An emphasis on building social capital recognizes the quality of information that results from positive and satisfying social networks and relationships. Quantum Leaders know that to increase positive social capital they make a choice to attend to every interaction as an investment in emotional, strategic, and spiritual rewards.

Chapter 5 (What You See Is Not What You Get) addresses the many unseen forces that we need to understand as negotiators. The structural interdependence created through globalization and modernization has an impact on our collective insecurity and anxiety more than ever. Our social reality is shaped by numerous invisible forces such as interconnectivity, demographic shifts, migration patterns, financial systems, goods and services, and the human nervous system.

The complexity of external forces and developments imposes stress and volatility on the nervous system of individuals, families, and social systems. We introduce the often-invisible forces that a Quantum Negotiator begins to observe. Much of the reality for negotiators is the knowledge that what we perceive is made up of incredibly small particles and forces that are generally unseen and not really perceivable on a day-to-day basis. We raise awareness about the small, the intractable, the unseen, and the invisible elements on which negotiation is based. We also share stories of how to pay attention to these forces and how to prevent derailing success and the ability to get what we need.

Chapter 6 (Leading Is Not about the Leader) concludes our exploration and focuses on the disruptive and rapidly changing environment for leaders today. Leadership is minimally effective with command and control but is more about creating social resonance and having a positive magnetic, motivating effect as a leader, which requires a deliberate quantum approach.

Throughout, we will provide numerous examples and illustrations. They reflect the experiences of real Quantum Negotiators and leaders, although we have changed names and specific references to maintain confidentiality and keep the focus on the essentials. Along the way, you will come across questions from Wendy, a typical hardball negotiator, and Thomas, a self-doubting negotiator, which are meant to spark your thinking. Toward the end of the book you will also discover how Paula, Martin, and Lina were able to transform their experiences and achieve surprising results by applying the principles of Quantum Negotiation.

Welcome to the Quantum Negotiation journey and the art of getting what you need!

PART

I

Quantum Negotiation Practice

1

The WHO & WHY of Quantum Negotiation

Harvey was an experienced baby boomer executive for a global manufacturer entering an important M&A negotiation with a digital software company. He had planned extensively around WHAT his targets, limits, and issues were. He put these in context of what he believed Kip, a millennial negotiator for the digital software company, would want. Harvey had always prepared for the Plan B or BATNA (Best Alternative to a Negotiated Agreement) in every negotiation not only regarding himself but also his counterpart.

On the day of their last negotiation to tie up the agreement, Harvey "lost his cool" and became very angry with Kip. Harvey's manufacturing company wanted to keep Kip on as a partner to integrate digitization for their global products. After many discussions, none of the "extremely generous" offers motivated Kip to sign the agreement to turn over his software company for integration into the manufacturing one.

Harvey was taken off guard by this young "upstart" and was offended that his financial offers were not valued. He had gone to great lengths to give Kip an offer—raising the salary and increasing bonuses for hitting digitization milestones. He made it clear to Kip that he was outraged by Kip's idea to create "happiness committees" around the integration process—he had never heard of such a thing and wasn't about to let his company get distracted by such nonsense. He couldn't believe that Kip was not at all motivated by an impressive substantial salary, financial security, or a new office and desk.

Harvey really needed this deal to work. The next best alternative was not very good and would be much too time consuming. He had to make this work with Kip.

★ ★ ★

Anchoring Equilibrium and Achieving Buoyancy

As a sociocentric leader, a Quantum Negotiator leads and negotiates through human impact. The anchor and clarity of their self-interests in the context of their relationships allows them to have a clear understanding of shared needs. Though it may seem obvious initially, it isn't quite as simple as you delve into it. To know what you need and want, why you need it, and how to get it is to know WHO you are on a deeper level.

Quantum Negotiators prepare themselves on five dimensions of their full human experience:

1. Cognitive Dimension: Thinking
2. Emotional Dimension: Feeling
3. Social Dimension: Behaving
4. Physical Dimension: Performing
5. Spiritual Dimension: Believing

The path to anchoring ourselves is grounded by awareness of these dimensions. The ultimate goal is to find equilibrium among all five human dimensions in order to be clear about our own and our counterpart's self-interests and to be buoyant enough to style-shift.

Cognitive

Preparing yourself on the cognitive level requires improvement of your analytical thinking skills and enhancement in your evaluation of competing interests and issues in a negotiation. The emphasis is on the ability to identify your goals and to cement your strategies prior to entering into a negotiation by asking the right questions of both yourself and your counterparts. Quality systematic preparation is key to getting what you want.

Emotional

The ability to identify and manage both your own and your counterparts' emotions effectively during a negotiation is indispensable. Proficiency in the emotional dimension not only allows you to identify and understand your own feelings and motivations during a negotiation, but it also helps you to better manage those of your counterparts. This enhanced understanding allows you to predict and defuse potentially detrimental situations. Taking the time prior to the negotiation to ground yourself and deal with any anxieties will go a long way, and will help you to best communicate what you want and to understand your counterparts.

Social

The social dimension requires discipline and preparation regarding your behavior with others. The skills associated with this dimension also include how to enhance and protect your reputation as a professional by working with your counterparts—not against them—to achieve a mutually beneficial solution. This reputation for trustworthiness and cooperation is a key quality of a Quantum Negotiator, who is mindful of coercive tactics and how ineffective they are in the context of complex relationships.

Physical

Physical preparation is as important as mental preparation for the negotiation process. Negotiation requires a significant expenditure of emotional and physical energy to get desired results, thus a healthy lifestyle is essential to negotiation effectiveness. Working out, eating well, and getting regular sleep are part of the discipline and practices of a Quantum Negotiator. Quantum Leaders understand that these practices can improve negotiation performance.

Spiritual

Getting what you want from a negotiation means nothing if you use tactics and behaviors that run contrary to your values, beliefs, and sense of purpose. Quantum Leaders are able to recognize the broader purpose and meaning that a negotiation has for them. They understand that classic coercive tactics are not merely ineffective, but also not in alignment with their sense of purpose, meaning, and connectivity with others in their lives. Figure 1.1 illustrates the way clarity on all the human dimensions can anchor negotiators.

Buoyancy

Buoyancy is having the awareness and clarity about the needs of a negotiator in all five human dimensions. Being aware of and anchoring the five human dimensions ensures that the Quantum Leader has all the necessary skills and experience to meet challenges faced when sharing resources, creating new opportunities, and getting things done. When Quantum Leaders have anchored equilibrium among all five human dimensions, they can be buoyant and can style-shift to build trust with their counterparts. Leaders are

Figure 1.1   The Quantum Negotiation Anchor.
©2015 Quantum Negotiation

in a negotiation when they have something they need and have to work with others to accomplish it. Leaders negotiate all the time under constant demands and limited time and resources.

The Quantum Leader is like a buoy designed for resilience; it is able to right itself in turbulence. Buoys function as markers—signs that help navigators get where they want to go by demarcating both safe and dangerous lanes of travel. The buoy, weighted at the bottom, is kept afloat by the force exerted upward by the weight of the water it displaces. With all its weight essentially concentrated in the bottom, the buoy becomes upended. It is designed to withstand environmental turbulence—wind, waves, tidal currents, the wakes of ships, and storms. The buoy is designed to right itself even during a period of extreme turbulence. It always pops back upright to serve its purpose and fulfill its function.

Quantum Leaders are buoyant. With each of the five human dimensions fully anchored and in balance, such leaders are not disrupted by turbulence and can right themselves after being tossed around, and steadfastly perform the job assigned. Quantum Leaders know the goal and how to reach it. They understand that they may potentially be intended victims of coercive or otherwise unfair tactics, but they know how to navigate this disturbance. If a Quantum Negotiator is off balance in one of the five human dimensions, successful negotiation is often unlikely. Therefore, mindfulness and reflection on these human factors becomes an important strategic requirement.

Why Does Negotiation Often Cause Such Strong Reactions within Us?

As soon as something becomes labeled as negotiation, powerful forces tend to get activated that are not otherwise activated.

When negotiating, we think very quickly about ourselves and our own self-interests. We start making assumptions about our counterparts' intentions—they are trying to take something away from us. As a result we start to feel vulnerable and get self-protective, and our focus turns inward. The instinctive "fight or flight" response is activated, and we either try to beat our counterparts, or avoid negotiation altogether. Filled with defensiveness and fear, our emotions can quickly boil over.

We feel vulnerable on multiple levels. On the physical dimension, our bodies can get stressed out. On the spiritual dimension, we may feel that our goals are being threatened. On the social dimension, we may feel a sense of alienation and conflict. These feelings add to the pressures that we can feel when negotiating, and cause us to behave in ways that we normally would not.

In fact, this response is what many negotiation courses exploit. They actually work with and feed that anxiety, essentially saying they'll teach you tricks and tactics and so on. This may temporarily work because they're exploiting the psychological state you're in when making snap assumptions about the other and become insecure about your own skills.

Leaders who understand how egoistic fear and negative emotions could drive them to accommodate, attack, or shy away from challenging situations develop reflection practices to prepare for stressful negotiations. By recognizing egoistic self-interest, Quantum Negotiators can manage the emotions, social dissonance, and physical tension in negotiation. Quantum Leaders are able to transform their thinking to be more interdependent, connected, and positive about shared self-interests in their personal and professional relationships.

Laughter and Negotiation

We don't easily associate negotiation with laughter; and if we do, it is tense, nervous laughter. For good reason. Negotiation is generally seen as a serious, relatively formal undertaking, that can induce a significant level of stress due to presumed antagonism, conflict, and some degree of distrust. Perhaps because it is such serious business, laughter can help stakeholders achieve breakthroughs at the emotional, relational, and also substantive level.

Laughter is, after all, a quintessential human characteristic with amazing benefits. Many scientific studies conclude that stress hormones decrease and don't allow for active prefrontal decision making. The immune system works better and changes brain wave activity toward what's called a "gamma frequency," amping up memory and recall, not only for individuals, but an entire group wanting to engage in a positive way. This leads to better memory, creativity, and tolerance for differences in problem solving while coping with daily stressors and anxieties.

Laughter is also a rather complex social occurrence that helps people bond, deal with stress together, and deepen their sense of connectedness. Most laughter in day-to-day interactions does not result from purposefully recounted jokes, but rather spontaneous witty and humorous remarks and/or playful behavior. Wit and puns, for instance, can help us shift perspective on otherwise serious issues, or simply enlarge the perspective on the situation we find ourselves in, reminding us of the bigger picture. Humor and playfulness help create a "natural" (or perhaps better: social) "high" by activating the same reward centers in the brain that are linked with happiness and drug-induced euphoria. This can help us reassess an issue and positively transform our experience of the moment. When people relax, daydream, joke around together, they engage in a mutual shift in their individual and connected brains to an "open" state of mind. This allows seeing others in a new way and puts perspectives and variables together as new possibilities, opening up opportunities previously precluded or unconceived—that is the true definition of creativity and of innovation.

Of course, not all humor generates these positive effects. Humor that aims to insult, belittle, or stereotype can have the exact opposite effect; it can sharply decrease feelings of connectedness, social support, and increase stress levels.

Most of us implicitly understand the effects of positive and negative humor. And, perhaps because the line between the two types can be blurry and highly subjective, we tend to avoid humor and playfulness altogether unless we are among friends and/or in situations where we feel comfortable and safe. But we rarely think of leading with humor to proactively transform tense and stressful situations to achieve a better outcome for all. Purposefully injecting humor and playfulness into negotiations can unlock a virtuous chain reaction with specific benefits:

1. Reduce stress experienced by all stakeholders involved, which helps:
   a. Create a more conducive sense of solidarity among the negotiating parties, including the willingness to trust, relate with empathy and an open mind, which enables
   b. Collaborative and creative problem solving that leads to previously unconceived opportunities and innovation for all parties involved.

One Quantum Leader and negotiator who we interviewed talks about it this way:

> I always try to bring some humor to my business interactions, particularly client relationships and negotiations. We are often too serious about it all and give it a weightiness that obscures the human dimension. We mask our insecurities and vulnerabilities, we make mistakes, overlook something, misspeak, do not clearly understand or comprehend. When we pierce through this with lightheartedness and an eye for the comic elements of everyday life, we shift the energy and atmosphere around us almost in a palpable, instantaneous, and irresistible way that draws people in and opens up new possibilities. But it cannot be shtick or a manipulative technique—people see through this a mile away. It has to be fueled by an authentic desire to build relationships on the level of play that is so much part of our essential nature.

All of us can probably attest to the magnetic and viral nature of playfulness. It has been described as a spiritual practice and reverse martial art. Cultivating humor and playfulness as part of how we relate and transform the social energy as we negotiate and lead may well be the essence of the quantum negotiator's "magic." Wielding it depends on our courage to uncover and rediscover our inner, playful nature and allowing it to inspire situations that are not typically associated with humor and play.

Assuming Responsibility

Thomas Asks:

What are the first steps I can take to be a better negotiator and get what I need?

Caring for your own self-interest is a major goal for a Quantum Negotiator. The pursuit of self-interest is a core human motivation that is often considered the primary reason humans need to acquire power. Understanding self-interest is essential in a negotiation. Quantum Negotiators affirm their own interests in a way that allows them to accomplish their goals without undermining the trust of their counterparts. They also examine how egoistic and controlling behaviors are ineffective for the complex personal and professional problems faced by leaders today.

Quantum Leaders explore an expanded definition of interdependent self-interest. This is particularly important when negotiating with a counterpart who becomes controlling and coercive. Classic coercive approaches have a long history, particularly in military and political campaigns. As in the past, there are still many high-profile political, economic, and business negotiators who thrive on pure self-interest and coercion to maximize gains. Without a more complex understanding of your self-interests and the compatibility of interests with a counterpart, it is often difficult to practice the Quantum Negotiation approach.

When Quantum Negotiators are clear about their self-interest, they enable themselves to begin a conscious exploration of the cognitive, emotional, social, physical, and spiritual dimensions of their own life. The key is to be clear about the people, activities, and values that matter most to you and your interests. We cannot accommodate everyone. Understanding deeper needs and trade-offs, and knowing how to say "no," are disciplines that require practice. The skills of a Quantum Negotiator are generated to identify their own needs and boundaries and to create greater freedom to be who they truly are. Quantum Leaders can fulfill their positive intentions and the true purpose of their leadership in interdependent relationships and teams.

The Risk of Accommodation

Thomas Asks:

OK, but I am a nice person. How can I still be nice and not get taken advantage of?

Accommodating and always giving in can be ineffective for leaders. Leaders often don't know where the line is between giving up too much or too little. With little clarity and recognition of our own needs, self-interests, and rights to those desires, there is a risk of accommodating or giving in on getting your own interests met. Often leaders may not be aware of the personal and professional consequences of too much accommodation.

When you ground yourself with the anchor, establish a clear vision, and develop buoyancy as a Quantum Negotiator, you are accommodating enough to negotiate, but you refrain from giving up on meeting your own needs. With a weak approach, there is no room for mutual gain. With a Quantum Negotiation mindset you can negotiate with a calm and open mind without being a pushover.

The process of becoming comfortable with the uncomfortable takes time, but it is crucial to a Quantum Negotiator's success—when you do this you are buoyant even while being tossed around in the sea of strong currents. Giving up on advocating for your own interests (or only advocating for your own interests) tests your counterpart, as it creates an imbalance with his or her needs and interests. The most successful negotiations are the balance of your needs and your counterpart's needs in the form of a partnership or relationship.

Sometimes you may feel opposed by a friend or coworker—in other words, someone who is not an "enemy," but someone you respect, value, and trust. To go against this person in a negotiation feels imbalanced and unhinges your own anchor of integrity. These situations are the ones that require you to be not only the clearest in your communication, but also buoyant.

Quantum Negotiators check their own emotional and social conditioning so that they can be more open and cooperative, rather than overly anxious to accommodate. This allows them to avoid capsizing in challenging relationships.

Accommodation, or avoiding conflict, is difficult in negotiation because it often hinders the journey to becoming a powerful Quantum Negotiator. Giving in can be seen as a way to resist coercive methods. You cannot become an effective and respected leader with accommodating or coercive behavior. Quantum Negotiators do not turn the other cheek or roll over and surrender. If they are up against a coercive adversary, they will not accommodate without a reciprocal concession. Their anchoring and buoyant presence sends a powerful signal to a counterpart. They are signaling that a counterpart cannot coerce them or drown them.

★ ★ ★

In order to prepare for critical thinking and analysis for negotiation, we will explore here the cognitive skills required for the contradictions, paradoxes, and complex social and political environments that Quantum Negotiators face.

How to Anchor Your Thinking—The Cognitive Dimension

Improvement in critical and paradox thinking increases the level of confidence and the likelihood of positive outcomes for negotiators. With systematic thinking, planning, and analysis, anyone can develop and improve their analytic negotiation capabilities and learn the common strategies and tactics that underlie most negotiations. An unlimited number of variables can affect negotiations, as each situation presents unique and challenging circumstances. But no matter what a negotiator's level of expertise, the dynamics of an actual negotiation can be analyzed and understood with some basic analytic tools. There are many variables that you need to prepare for; some of these variables are personal and some of them concern your counterpart. The QN preparation checklist systematically outlines these variables. For a more detailed list for preparation see page 78 in Part II Quantum Negotiation Tools.

Expect the Unexpected

Anyone who has engaged in negotiation knows to expect the unexpected. You can be blindsided by an adversary in a variety of ways, whether by coercive tactics, aggressive behavior, or even by an offer that seems too good to be true. Every negotiator takes the occasional unexpected salvo. It is how you respond to the hit that is important. Expecting the unexpected is a skill that requires facility and integration of our full human experience. Withstanding the turbulence that results from the unexpected and being able to right yourself during the period of unsettled activity is the test of a Quantum Negotiator. When you can manage your mind, your emotions, and your behavior and respond appropriately, you are buoyant. Quantum Leaders move from egoistic to sociocentric thinking, and move from rigid to buoyant in their behavior. They are more resistant, present, and satisfied with their life and work experiences.

Set and Prioritize Your Goals

This stage of preparation is critical to determine the facts and issues that define your goals; it is also important to be clear about your underlying interests, and those of the stakeholders you represent in the negotiation. You must gather sufficient information in order to prioritize your long-term strategic and short-term immediate goals. This process determines how you will measure success, and highlights the information you need to examine further.

Be as clear and specific as you can about what you need and want. Link your goals to realistic standards but also reach for, expect, and commit yourself to the best opportunities.

You also must take the time to discover as much as you can about the goals and interests of your counterpart. The strength of the two parties' compatible interests and the potential for a long-term relationship are at the core of Quantum Negotiation. Disciplined reflection and exploration about the interdependent nature of the relationship and the ways in which the parties can meet or reinforce each other's interests can lead to optimal results. This framework critically increases the buoyancy and Quantum Leadership required for a negotiated outcome with mutual gains.

Research Substantive Information

Negotiators who keep their eyes and ears open know that gathering intelligence is a basic human skill. In today's information-saturated environment, it's easier than ever to gain knowledge and insight into your counterpart's likely goals and objectives, as well as the internal organizational and external environmental factors that motivate them. With effective insights about the overall conditions driving their counterparts, negotiators will have the confidence, information, and skills necessary to apply Quantum Leadership principles and manage inevitable surprises. Furthermore, the Quantum Negotiator willingly explores his or her counterpart's interests, rather than just their positions, and so she or he is best positioned to be cocreative in brainstorming about options and mutually beneficial outcomes.

Enhance Intelligence Gathering

Being well-connected in today's information environment is a great way to enhance the emotional and social engagement required to implement an effective negotiation strategy and to remain adaptable to potential changes—after all, a good plan is only as good as the ability to shift strategic direction. The ability to shift strategic direction in a negotiation so that you can greater influence and collaborate with others is known as *style-shifting*. The social dimension of Quantum Negotiation explores the behavioral and cultural styles of your counterparts in order to practice style-shifting.

In addition to the demand for more up-to-date and canny insight, today's fast-changing pace creates progressively more demand for cross-cultural social skills. Thus, for a Quantum Negotiator, a successful individual or organizational negotiation plan can only be achieved when there is an integrated approach of analytical, emotional, and social insight and information.

Embracing the Left and Right Brain

You must also learn to understand the role our brains play during negotiation. A disciplined understanding of how the brain processes both strategic information and emotional elements yields more constructive relationships and outcomes in negotiation.

A Quantum Negotiator who can help others explore a broader range of interests and motivations, and who can engage them in a problem-solving process, can create more opportunities for problem solving. According to social neuroscience research, facilitation is a talent accomplished by leveraging the system of brain interconnectedness and the coordination of left and right brain hemispheres. When interpersonal competencies are built on specific neural circuits and related systems that inspire others to be effective and cooperative, the power to influence others is increased.

Coordinating left and right brain functions requires disciplined attention, nurturing, and practice. These exercises are required to facilitate the use of neural pathways in the brain. Quantum Negotiators practice these new behaviors, which start with a commitment to pay attention to how our brains work. Begin to understand the values and preferences stored in your brain.

Wendy Asks:

How can I work out my brain so that the two sides function together?

A good way to start is to welcome coaching and feedback to increase ways you can articulate your dreams and goals to others. Listen and understand others with more attention. This careful attention can help overcome bad habits of coercion. Awareness about how your brain functions helps you work against the thickness of the brain circuitry created over your life time, which may be causing a coercive behavior—it is often an unconscious habit. By doing this, you can build new neural pathways in your brain. This will help you become more flexible, adaptable, and creative.

Utilizing our whole brain can be a powerful tool in problem solving, particularly in complex and ambiguous situations. Neither intricate personal negotiations nor critical contract negotiations can be managed solely with logical, linear, computer-like thinking. Such negotiations also require the key skills of self-knowledge, empathy, and detection of subtleties in human interaction. Although emotional and social intelligence have historically been ignored or suppressed in negotiation education, social and emotional skills now serve as fundamental features of a Quantum Negotiator.

Quantum Leaders are mindful that nonverbal messages are being sent. The next step is to be able to decode nonverbal messages effectively. The development of both right and left hemispheres of the brain is essential for negotiation planning. If, for example, you are a more linear thinker (left), you can practice with more creative ideas and endeavors (right), or vice versa. Both are essential to human reasoning, social interactions, and successful negotiation processes. The biological underpinning occurs when negotiators consciously or unconsciously detect and attune to another's emotions in a negotiation. This social and emotional awareness is a powerful way to leverage brain interconnectedness.

Skilled negotiation requires the practice of observation—specifically, observing how your unconscious messages and those of others are being decoded throughout negotiation interactions. These unconscious messages can be ineffective. Quantum Negotiators have long practiced strengthening the left side of the brain with more analytic, strategic, and cognitive planning skills. Today Quantum Negotiators include a practice to increase the right-side capabilities, which tend toward more creativity and attempt to tap into the engagement of emotional and social motivations.

How to Anchor Your Emotions—The Emotional Dimension

The emotional dimension involves the need to recognize and manage your feelings in a negotiation so that you can achieve an optimal outcome. The objective is to manage your emotions to work *for* you, not *against* you. You also want to be able to identify and manage your counterpart's emotional responses.

The emotional dimension builds on an in-depth understanding of emotional intelligence. The basic building blocks of emotional intelligence can help you accurately perceive, evaluate, and regulate your own emotions. On the surface, this may seem like a relatively simple task, but you may have to do considerable digging to understand the feelings and emotions you experience in negotiation.

A Quantum Negotiator focuses on learning how to identify, manage, and trust his or her own emotions, which then leads others to cooperate and coordinate effectively, thus facilitating negotiation.

The fundamental skills required to achieve balance in the emotional dimension are the ability to recognize the feeling of being caught up in emotions such as anger, fear, and intolerance, and the power to keep yourself from getting swept away by them. By acknowledging, managing, and trusting your own emotions, you become more aware of your feelings and can interpret emotional responses in someone else. As you become more self-aware, you will see how your own emotions color your view of your counterpart.

A Quantum Leader will develop a high level of self-awareness and the ability to monitor his or her reactions. They can observe their feelings and behaviors during negotiating sessions and use emotions to their advantage. Proper preparation can prevent emotions from derailing engagement with a counterpart. Quantum Leaders learn to take a more objective view and can constructively lead others as a result. Managing emotions makes it possible to connect with others, share resources, and expand problem-solving opportunities in negotiation, even when there is conflict.

For example, an inexperienced leader might become anxious about a salary negotiation. With a more systematic understanding of industry benchmarks and the value they offer the organization, these inexperienced leaders will be able to best work through their anxieties and insecurities, eventually arriving at a fair agreement. By combining important information and a better understanding of their anxieties with attention to the strategic skills to manage those fears, inexperienced negotiators can respond to problems and generate options during intimidating salary negotiations.

A Quantum Negotiator knows that emotions are produced by an interaction of thoughts, physiological changes, and behaviors that occur in response to external events. Basic human needs are often at risk when trying to create something new, share a resource, or close a contract, thus emotional responses can be expected. The suppression of emotions deprives you of valuable information about yourself and prevents you from finding integration and balance among the five human dimensions.

The main components for developing proficiency in emotional intelligence are to observe yourself and to understand the relationships between your thoughts and feelings, and your reactions. The emotional skills required to handle stress, to understand other people's feelings and concerns, and to take responsibility for your own decisions and actions can be developed more easily once you accept and understand your own feelings and moods.

Learning about Your Counterpart

For Quantum Negotiators, a quality relationship is key to creating workable agreements. You could spend a lifetime observing another person without ever fully understanding them; it is in your best interest to develop strategic preparation methods in order to learn about your counterparts so that you can support their goals as well as your own. This can be difficult but it is not impossible.

Quantum Leadership uses value creation methods rather than control to share or expand limited resources. When an investigation includes learning about a counterpart's needs and concerns, a Quantum Negotiator is more likely to encourage others to engage and to cooperate. When negotiators recognize that they often have compatible emotional and substantive needs, they see that their self-interests are shared or sociocentric; this empowers the leaders to collaborate to achieve their mutual goals.

Emotional Intelligence Practices

Emotional intelligence practices can elicit vital information about your counterparts' needs and motivations. These practices can increase your social engagement in a negotiation and make it easier to address the parties' interdependent needs. These practices are also critical to a cooperative and satisfying social engagement process.

Predatory practices in the classic tradition are considered deceitful, inappropriate, and often illegal or immoral today. These tactics can result in the destruction of sustainable agreements in both personal and professional negotiations. Preying on a counterpart's weaknesses could destroy the relationship and your reputation. When a facilitative, rather than manipulative, Quantum Leader wants to enhance power in order to get others to cooperate, the first step is to develop skills in emotional intelligence using the following tools.

The Skill of Observation

When a negotiation fails, it is often due to an inability to read social and emotional signals. One way to gather key information about your counterpart is through disciplined observations, made when you are communicating with them verbally and nonverbally.

Emotional intelligence skills include being able to enhance working relationships with others, attention and skill in identifying and serving others' needs, and being able to manage conflicts and encourage inclusiveness and collaboration with teams. Social skills in observing what others need and what information they may possess can increase your ability to gather critical information. These observation skills can be utilized before and during a negotiation.

Developing emotional and social observation skills enables you to notice the fine details about your daily interactions with others. As you shift away from the habitual, unconscious, or reflexive negotiation practices of defensiveness, egoism, and coercion to practices of understanding, you begin to sense the emotional and social subtext inherent in the interpersonal negotiation dynamic.

Social awareness involves, first, choosing to observe and sense others' feelings and perspectives and second, taking into account their interests and concerns. In addition, a choice is made to understand the issues, politics, and informal structure of the organizational and negotiation team culture that underlies the negotiation.

Thomas Asks:

It sounds like I have to cater a lot to my counterparts. Won't they sense this and try to take advantage of my interest in them?

This choice to anchor into a leadership position in a negotiation is the cornerstone of a Quantum Negotiator. This choice is to fully anchor yourself into realizing your full human potential. You can achieve this grounding by understanding your own emotions and interests more deeply, and then working constructively with others to achieve those goals.

Managing Destructive Emotions

Classic negotiation theorists have long warned leaders not to underestimate the danger of destructive emotions. Social neuroscientists have a scientific explanation of how this "brain-to-brain linkup" between negotiators works and how the contagion spreads. More importantly, psychologists and neuroscientists have provided us with ways to regulate the potential destructive aspects of our socially wired brains.

Negotiation creates an incubator for the spread of destructive emotions. Negotiations often represent a domain where aspirations and desires to increase one's own power can create intense competition and fear.

In addition, social engagement and exposure to others who have different values and beliefs often occur in the context of extreme competition for limited resources, placing all parties at risk of the ill effects of destructive emotions.

Wendy Asks:

How can you recognize and assess destructive emotions? Negotiation is by nature kind of abrasive.

The ability to recognize the impact of another person's anger and distress is necessary to maintain vitality as a negotiator. When negotiators succumb to destructive emotions, their power is weakened. People have a hard time thinking strategically when anxiety, resentment, or envy overtakes logic. Successful Quantum Leaders emphasize that it is strategically important to protect yourself against negative emotions. Negotiators who allow themselves to be affected by negativity put themselves at risk, because they often waste valuable time and resources trying to free themselves from the bad energy.

Develop Disputation Skills

Quantum Leaders often use effective disputation skills, which make them aware of any pessimistic reactions they have in a setback. These skills encourage constructive action. Quantum Leaders know that an effort should be made not to withdraw or lose energy after suffering a setback.

Emotional balance can help with focus and the ability to remain optimistic in order to plan for the next steps. Successfully managing your response to a setback may be something such as: *I may not have been at my best during the meeting. I was distracted and unprepared, but I will not make a catastrophe out of this situation. I will create a better negotiation plan. I'm thinking about new ideas to discuss at the next meeting in order to get their attention and hold their interest.*

How to Anchor Your Behavior—The Social Dimension

In order to prepare for increased social interaction and quality connections for partnerships in negotiation, we will explore here the social skills required to receive and give support to others and to cooperate rather than compete against others to achieve Quantum Negotiators results.

Calibrate Your Behavior

The social dimension of Quantum Negotiation involves the ways that you can support others and anticipate the impact of your behavior on them. This awareness provides guidance about your social intelligence and how to share goals, build bonds, and brainstorm solutions with counterparts. The objective is to improve your capacity for identifying cultural gaps and developing style-shifting behaviors for when you need to cooperate rather than compete against others.

Trust as a Factor of Reputation

Generating trust is highly valued in this social and interdependent context. A reputation for trustworthiness and collaboration has considerable value in professional and personal negotiations. The notion of a trustworthy reputation is in sharp contrast to the classic notion of intimidation as the major factor of a valuable reputation. When the problems are interconnected and require mutual coordination for a realistic solution, those who can engage positively with others generate a constructive social reputation for themselves.

In order to build positive social capital, you must share information, coordinate activities, and make good collective decisions. In a mutual-gains negotiation, a reputation of fear will not generate social cooperation. Attention to trust-enhancing behaviors will lead to social resonance, positive energy, and rapport within and across negotiation teams. This increases the potential for critical information sharing. Both parties must be aware of the ways that each can help the other to understand and solve problems.

In most leadership situations, the informal disclosure of information is required before effective action can be undertaken. Sustained positive social relationships and networks are the most effective way to gain access to useful information that might otherwise be hidden, because attention and time are limited resources.

A quality investment of time in relationship management contributes to an internal coherence for negotiation partnerships or groups. When agreements and relationships enhance a sustainable future for the contract and relationships, the value of your reputation increases significantly. Constructive social relationships improve negotiation outcomes and result in less costly dispute resolutions.

Developing Social Intelligence

The social dimension explores how to assess the nature of the contemporary social, political, and economic environment in which you will pursue your negotiations. It explains how power sources and centers have changed dramatically since classical times.

There remain, of course, tyrants with their small fiefdoms of centralized power who monopolize political and economic capital and intimidate with destructive tactics. But with the advent of social change and access to vital information and political and economic expertise, the nature of power has significantly changed. As Quantum Leaders, we can benefit from this democratization of the modern political economy.

Quantum Negotiators know that before they make a proposal, they need to find out whether, and why, others become positional or defensive in a negotiation. If you want others to cooperate, it is important to anticipate any coercive and hardened position you may take so that you can prevent it.

Brainstorm with your team to generate a range of potential solutions that you might put forward during a negotiation. Applying cooperation skills, investing in social capital, and developing social intelligence may seem easy, but you need to become aware of those skills that you practice unconsciously. Once Quantum Negotiators learn these natural skills, and develop and practice them, their negotiations become more cooperative, and they achieve greater balance among all five human dimensions.

How to Anchor Your Performance—The Physical Dimension

The physical dimension of a Quantum Negotiation involves ways that you can negotiate with more energy, resilience, and clarity.

One of the keys to a powerful performance presence is the ability to project a strong physical presence that will draw power and attention to you. A Quantum Leader develops discipline around an optimistic mindset, physical stewardship, energy recovery, and sound nutrition as part of their negotiation preparation. Often there is a lack of physical and emotional energy, which are often debilitated by cynicism, apathy, and irritability; however, Quantum Negotiators make the choice to establish habits of high physical performance to change their outlook and presence to become buoyant.

In most cases, physical energy can be enhanced by the discipline of an optimistic mindset. But in some cases, structural, neurological, or physical injuries may complicate this practice. If you or someone you know is in constant pain and distress in social interactions, medical attention may be needed before they can begin to improve their performance. Depleted physical strength can impair the focus and attention required for sustainable, high-performance practices. Quantum Negotiation requires healthy reflection, physical resilience, and stamina. It takes significant physical and emotional energy to style-shift, adapt, and influence others in complex cultural and economic settings.

When your brain is fatigued, or lacking oxygen or hydration, you become impatient and unable to foster the physical stamina and energy required in a negotiation. If you are relatively inexperienced or need to negotiate with a coercive negotiator, you can benefit from increased stamina and clarity. It is useful to review your presumptions about your physical stamina and how you plan to manage the fatigue and lack of clarity that can undermine your performance. Attention to your physical stamina sharpens the quality of your thinking and behavior in social interaction, particularly during a stressful negotiation.

Quantum Leaders are successful negotiators who thrive in situations of uncertainty and limited resources. The leaders who make a conscious choice to develop the habits of a sustainable performer for buoyancy—just as athletes train for sports—are the most successful. Some steps from Tignum's, Sink, Float, or Swim, outlined here will help increase your stamina and help you achieve a positive performance mindset and ability to style-shift.

Performance Nutrition

Practicing performance nutrition means purposefully choosing food that improves energy, resilience, and brain performance in order to develop the focus and clarity that produce sustainable negotiation stamina. Use nutrition strategies to increase your energy by limiting your intake of sugar and carbohydrates. This keeps blood glucose stable and prevents mood swings. Reduce the chemicals, preservatives, hydrogenated oils, and trans fats in your diet. Make sure that the fats you eat are healthy ones.

Performance Movement

Performance movement means utilizing physical motion. Exercise to reduce pain, generate energy, increase resilience, improve brain performance, maximize capacity, and produce sustainable stamina for negotiation success. Establish an exercise routine. Walk regularly. Do strengthening movements at least three times per week.

Performance Recovery

Most people don't think about how much physical labor goes into negotiating, but when we stop and think about what negotiation entails, such as listening, analyzing, doing math, using the right vocabulary, managing our emotions, or composing or writing up documents with precision, we can safely say that it is generally one of the more exhausting things to do at work or during our day-to-day lives.

Performance recovery involves purposefully resting and regenerating to develop energy, resilience, and brain performance. It also involves the capacity to enhance passion and purpose for negotiation success. Plan for recovery time when you recognize your energy is depleted and you feel irritable and ineffective. Implement relaxation and exercise techniques into your planning for long days of negotiation and problem solving. Use progressive relaxation. Take power naps and do breathing exercises to re-energize. Be aware of the way recovery improves your creativity, energy, and focus for buoyancy in a negotiation.

How to Anchor Your Beliefs—The Spiritual Dimension

Thomas Asks:

I have beliefs, but I wouldn't call myself spiritual. Are you suggesting that I join a religion or develop faith in a god?

Practice Spiritual Intelligence

The practice of spiritual intelligence and the pursuit of mutual gains increase the sense of purpose, satisfaction, and meaning in a negotiation. Spiritual intelligence is most broadly defined as the knowledge with which we access our deepest sense of meaning and purpose, as well as our highest motivations. Today's Quantum Negotiators face complex problems that require brain capacities beyond the scope of left-brain logic and linear calculations. Proficiency in negotiation today involves preparation on the cognitive level as well as on the emotional, social, physical, and spiritual levels. Leaders need to reach beyond the limits of cognition by paying attention to the spiritual dimension of negotiation. This kind of preparation enhances the motivation and discipline required for Quantum Negotiation.

A negotiation can involve a conscious choice to activate the temporal lobe's sources of purpose and connectivity instead of the primal fear that comes from the brain's amygdala. Spiritual practices, such as reflection, prayer, and meditation, can enhance performance of the body and the brain. These practices strengthen neural function in specific parts of the brain that reduce anxiety and increase neuroplasticity, thus preventing deterioration of brain function. Such brain health is necessary for the social awareness, empathy, and improved analytic function required for creative problem solving.

Conscious connection with one's belief system and behavioral flexibility is critical in order to adjust behavior instantly without compromising one's integrity or dignity. Given the constraints of limited preparation time, most negotiators need to rely on increased emotional, social, and spiritual capacities in a fast-paced environment. Quantum Negotiators excel when they are able to monitor and adjust their emotions and behaviors in ambiguous situations. A strict analytical plan to control these forces has little utility.

Conscious assessment of what provides meaning and purpose, however, guides the management of emotions and social behavior. This integration increases a negotiator's sense of power and confidence in the pursuit of personal and professional goals. Mediocre negotiators tend to resist switching from coercive power to a conscious, reflective mode of thinking under conditions of ambiguity or threat.

The development of facilitation and problem-solving skills requires an ability to confront and work through defensiveness and habitual coercive practices. As negotiators become more mindful of their own values and desires to be treated with dignity, "they develop an internal state of peace that comes with the recognition and acceptance of the value and vulnerability of all living beings."

This power to understand the universal desire for dignity increases the clarity, balance, and buoyancy to lead others in turbulent and ambiguous situations. When negotiators treat others with dignity, they become more connected and are able to create more meaningful relationships in order to problem solve and share limited resources.

The more intensely you focus on understanding a greater purpose, the more positive your interaction with others will be. This optimism brings about decreased activity in the parietal lobe, which affects our sense of self. Through meditation and prayer, the ego can dissolve into a greater sense of connection with others. "Contemplation . . . of spiritual values appears to permanently change the structure of those parts of the brain that control moods, give rise to our conscious notions of self, and shape our sensory perceptions of the world." Then later, "contemplative practices strengthen a specific neurological circuit that generates peacefulness, social awareness, and compassion for others."

Conscious efforts of mindfulness and reflection serve as active modes of cognition that play important roles in complex problem solving. Put some spiritual principles into action. Practicing principles such as forgiveness, compassion, gratitude, thankfulness, and service to others can activate stronger neural circuits. With focus on and practice of spiritual principles, they become habitual in your life activities. This mindful change can lead to the action and outcomes that Quantum Negotiators want to achieve.

★ ★ ★

Let's return to Harvey and Kip.

Harvey expressed his frustration about the possibility of losing this deal with his Quantum Negotiation coach. He came to realize that he had prepared for WHAT he wanted and HOW he was going to get it, but he had neglected to explore WHO his counterpart was.

Harvey began to explore WHO Kip was and what his needs really were—even though Harvey could not understand them at first. After reviewing this as part of his preparation, Harvey began to genuinely explore what Kip needed at the next meeting. Harvey discovered that Kip needed to see a transparent and collaborative work environment during the integration process. Harvey's experience was that integration was usually a highly contentious process, but he began to see how this critical element could be more engaging. Harvey also began to understand that Kip did not need a formal desk or position; rather, he wanted open and flexible decision making in which everyone's opinions would matter.

Because of his patience in exploring Kip's needs, Harvey could see the connection to his own need for a successful integration, which could be enhanced with Kip's. Kip had significant forward thinking ideas and liked collective problem solving, inclusion, quality relationships, and satisfaction at work. Kip welcomed any coaching and guidance he could get from Harvey and they both began to educate each other. They not only signed the deal, but also created an engaging integration team. They discovered that they both wanted to belong to a winning organization they could be proud of and maximize their own performance in the future. Harvey began to approach his role in a more fulfilling and enjoyable way.

Summary: Stay Anchored and Grounded

Before you begin your negotiation, you must first understand WHO you are and WHO your counterpart is. What are your goals in the negotiation? What are the facts and issues that define your goals? What are your underlying interests? What are your priorities, in relation to short- and long-term goals? How do you measure success? When you understand who you are, ask these same questions about your counterpart.

Once you see the WHO, you need to ask the WHY. Why are you in this relationship—what is the purpose of the negotiation? What are your needs and concerns? Why is success important to both you and your counterpart? What are the tangible and intangible needs and desires of both parties? What are the cross-cultural factors that influence why you are both here and negotiating?

Being prepared is the most important part of any negotiation, and the success of both parties depends on it. If you are missing any of the WHO or WHY, do not begin before you understand.

2

The WHAT & WHAT IF of Quantum Negotiation

Dr. Terry Garza is a research scientist for an international food organization. His organization's sole purpose is to develop methods to increase production of the developing world's food supply. His organization discovered a substance that, when added to the soil, dramatically reduces the amount of moisture needed in the soil to grow a variety of staple crops. It would effectively allow currently fallow and drought-parched land to grow crops. It also has the promise to slow the process of the land turning into desert ("desertification") and produce crops with less water, potentially saving millions of lives lost due to famine and drought.

This new substance can only be found in the Sri Lankan star fruit, which grows on trees in certain parts of Sri Lanka. The trees, which bear fruit only once every two years, are in a deserted and remote part of the country, making them highly inaccessible for easy harvesting. All efforts to transplant the trees or expand production have been unsuccessful. The process for obtaining the soil additive from the star fruit requires the seeds inside the star fruit to be turned into a fine powder.

Garza learned that the biannual harvest was completed and controlled by the Sri Lankan Ministry of Agriculture, which would sell the batch to the highest bidder. Knowing the importance of the powder and the potential lives that might be saved by using it in the right way, he was eager to purchase the next harvest. He was authorized by his organization to spend up to $2 million.

His excitement was tempered when he learned that he was not the only one interested in the star fruit harvest. His competition was Ecobil, one of the biggest and most successful biotech firms in the United States. Ecobil was a well-funded leader in genetic engineering processes, biomedical technology, and the creation of new products for the agricultural and health sciences. Garza set up a time to meet with one of their representatives, Dr. Anita Maxwell, to explain how important it was that he obtain the star fruit, and to dissuade her from making a bid.

When Garza met with Maxwell she told him that her firm had an annual multimillion-dollar budget for the development of new products. She had spent millions of dollars on the research and development of a new drug that would not only reduce blood cholesterol levels but also reduce cholesterol buildup. Unfortunately for Garza, the drug required a new substance that could only be found in the Sri Lankan star fruit. Maxwell was firm in her insistence that she would bid whatever was required to get the star fruit for Ecobil. Too much had been invested, and too much was at stake.

Garza and Maxwell's meeting became extremely tense as they both insisted they needed the supply of star fruit for their mission. The two-hour conversation was reduced to a volley between what each of them wanted—the star fruit. After an embarrassing shouting match, Garza remembered to find his quantum anchor to steady himself, took a deep breath, asked for a break, and took a short walk. He then remembered to think more carefully at why he needed the star fruit.

When Maxwell and Garza met again after a break, they both apologized for their anxious exchange and began to speak about the engineering process in which they would use the star fruit. Garza pointed out that his organization would be producing a soil additive, created when the seeds of the star fruit were pulverized into a fine powder. The powder from the seeds of an entire harvest would produce enough soil additive to reclaim land supporting more than twenty thousand people. When she heard this, Maxwell stood up from her chair and exclaimed that her new drug required the pulp but not the seeds from the fruit.

This was a real turning point for each of them as they excitedly agreed to make one bid to the Ministry and share the entire product— Maxwell's company would take the pulp and then share all the seeds with Garza's organization. They had forgotten to think about what they *needed* as opposed to what they *wanted*.

★ ★ ★

In terms of our quantum model, the first chapter was built around the question of who we are. This chapter delves into the question of what we want and why we want it.

Just like Dr. Garza and Dr. Maxwell, any negotiators become fixated on a particular goal—what it is we want, that number, that quality, that particular product—before ever really exploring why we have that goal and if it is what we truly need. When we enter a negotiation it becomes the focus for us and we never really challenge that. Just like the way the lens of a camera closes its aperture to focus in on a particular subject, when we focus in on a single goal, other possibilities become blurry and fade away into the background.

When we get stuck in this mindset, we lose out on a lot of opportunities to get that need met through different goals. Too prematurely we equate success with one particular thing. Our lens is too constricted to open ourselves up to other alternatives and get a clear picture of the context.

We tend to underestimate the intangible forces that are really driving the need to accomplish our goal. This is why in a quantum method we spend a lot of time on that unseen component that is driving our fixation toward that goal. We like to look at the cognitive dimension, the social dimension, and the emotional, physical, and spiritual dimensions. Once you get clarity on the unseen needs, the goal itself becomes crystal clear. It also becomes more flexible once you understand what is driving that need.

This is the difference between "the artful deal" and "the art of manipulating a deal." With "the art of manipulating a deal" you try to get people to relax so that you can impose your power upon them. It's about weakening the other, or reducing the vigilance of the other, so that you can build your surprise attack. It's a leveling technique, a way of opening up all of those human channels. This mindset assumes we need to show up as cunning. It's not about being a real, three-dimensional person; it's about being on guard and projecting a ferocious side of myself that is not who I am or who I ever want to be. A true manipulator working "the art of manipulating a deal" actually uses fear and closes the aperture, leaving others with very few ways to move because fear is being used against them.

In contrast, a Quantum Leader seeking "the artful deal" knows that fear exists and fear is in most negotiations. They open the aperture and facilitate a sense of safety in the context of this fear, and find that their power to influence is actually expanded as a result. They have created an artful setting for this kind of relationship.

We require psychological safety to be at our most motivated, engaged, and committed. It is from this state that the most innovative, value-creating solutions arise. However, the implicit, unconscious message around negotiation is that it's not psychologically safe. It's for this very reason that many people turn to manipulative tactics to inoculate themselves against feeling unsafe.

A Quantum Negotiator uses a different set of tactics that are not meant to coerce, but to build trust and psychological safety. Rather than aggressively asserting power, a Quantum Negotiator will spend time in the preliminary phase creating a positive relationship, encouraging curiosity, and jointly setting the agenda. We prefer to call these behavioral guidelines. Once you have practiced them enough, they become natural to who you are and are simply the way you show up.

★ ★ ★

Negotiation as a Battle

> ### Wendy Asks:
>
> I've always learned that negotiation is a battle, in which I need to use the best tactics to outmaneuver and dominate my opponent to win. If this idea is wrong, then why is it so widespread?

The conventional perspective of negotiation as a battle has its roots in a world with much more scarcity and much less possibility than today.

When Sun-Tzu developed *The Art of War* in the fourth century BC, and Niccolo Machiavelli produced his laws of power in the sixteenth century, entire nations or empires were ruled by one single king or emperor. In order to maintain control, these tyrants drew more power and attention to themselves by showing a tough physical presence. They played political games with their courtiers, using time-consuming maneuvers so as to appear threatening. They starved others of their attention so that they would crave even small concessions.

Of course, there are "tyrants" today with their small fiefdoms of centralized power who monopolize political and economic capital and intimidate others with destructive tactics. But this is rare today. With twenty-first-century social change and increasing access to political and economic expertise, the nature of power has changed significantly. We as negotiators now can engage others and benefit from a democratization of access and collaboration. Gaming others into traps is not very effective in leadership when colleagues, team members, or vendors have more access than ever to getting what they need—not only in terms of products and services, but also in satisfying customer and team relationships.

Most of us are not courtiers, military officers, or political ministers who fiercely compete for access to very limited elite economic, political, and social positions. The competition for power for us is not a vicious battle of all-or-nothing wins and losses. It was this way in the past, when the classic laws of power were designed. Power centers and sources were autocratic, highly controlled, and deadly competitive. The world today is much different.

In today's environment we need to develop relationships and wins with others to get what we want. Preparation does not mean mastery of a Machiavellian artifice to establish a powerful presence. Tactics such as "tough guy," "hide-and-seek," or "tricky games" often alienate others who want to be treated with respect and collaboration. There are more negotiators today who are changing the basic rules about how to develop a strong presence as a negotiator. Today, new rules and methods to establish a strong negotiation presence are from the world of sustainable high performance and human potential.

Most of us don't really have the time or capacity to learn the classic tricks even if they were successful. But when we are not prepared, we often default to the old classic notion that there are scarce resources and that if we don't win, we will lose. This creates a sense of powerlessness, frustration, and even despair. Eventually it will lead to physical and emotional burnout. That's the bad news—it's easy to default to classic tactics even though they get us nowhere.

The good news is that there are many examples of successful Quantum Negotiators who thrive in situations of uncertainty and limited resources even when the odds might be against them. The key is that those who do well as Quantum Negotiators make a conscious choice to understand their own anchors for buoyant performance under stress. This is much like the anchor to the sea floor for a buoyant ship. They develop disciplines around anchoring an optimistic mindset, physical stewardship, energy recovery, and emotional, social, and spiritual awareness about their own and others' needs. This supports a better understanding about what they and others want in a negotiation. It also provides insight about how to behave collaboratively with others to get what they need. Even those who have felt a lack of emotional and physical energy, who may have been debilitated by cynicism, apathy, or irritability, make the choice to establish habits of high performance to change their own outlook and presence.

Quantum Negotiators enhance their ability to understand and engage with others with an optimistic mindset. They are also aware that in some cases there are structural neurological or physical injuries that colleagues, family, or friends may experience. Quantum Leaders are mindful that someone may be in constant pain or distress in social interactions.

Depleted emotions and physical strength can impair one's ability to understand how many needs there are in negotiation. Quantum Negotiators prepare for healthy reflection, physical resilience, and stamina to explore what they need. They also offer attention to what others need to accomplish in a negotiation. Quantum Negotiators know that negotiation takes significant physical and emotional energy to understand others and to style-shift if needed.

Quantum Negotiators think of the ways that their mental clarity, performance, and physical presence are often drained. They also rest so that they can anchor themselves to be buoyant enough to get what they need—for example, if their brains are fatigued or lack oxygen or hydration, they will take a break and recharge. They are aware of how they become too impatient or irritable when thinking about others under stress.

The results of not exploring a counterpart can often lead to no results—unless you just get lucky. Joseph Duveen, a 1920s art dealer, is a great example of someone who was impatient to explore what his counterpart wanted in an upcoming negotiation. All Duveen heard was that his client, Henry Ford, was planning to purchase the "world's greatest art collection." Duveen had not discovered that Ford, although quite wealthy, had very modest tastes. In the end, Ford did not want to buy any of Duveen's superior paintings, but was thrilled with the colorful booklet of art reproductions Duveen brought to the negotiation. Duveen ultimately gave Ford the art book, and walked away from the negotiation empty-handed. Without understanding what his counterpart wanted or why he wanted it, this negotiator did not get what he needed.

Leverage—Necessary to Getting What You Want

Having leverage is an essential requirement for getting what you want when negotiating with others. The word "leverage" was originally used as a noun to indicate positional advantage over others in a negotiation. Quantum Leaders, however, think of leverage as a verb—to lift up or engage untapped, invisible mental, social, psychological, and spiritual resources. They understand leverage not as "power over" others but as "power with" others.

Thomas Asks:

It seems kind of counterintuitive to give the other party power in a negotiation setting. Can you give me an example of what you actually mean?

The root of the word is lever. A lever is used to elevate something by utilizing a very simple machine idea with a focal point or fulcrum that can be used to lift or move a load or weight. Even when Quantum Negotiators have thought they may be weak or vulnerable in a negotiation, they have been able to elevate themselves out of a powerless situation through Quantum preparation.

In that sense leverage is a tool to transform limited time and resources. In short, leverage can be understood by evaluating how much each party in a negotiation needs or wants from an agreement. More specifically, it is about how relative the needs are between the parties and what the consequences are if an agreement is not reached.

In negotiation, leverage is a measure of which party, at any given moment, needs the other party relatively more. Picture two graduate students in a negotiation—Jose, who is selling his car, and Ricardo, who is looking to buy one. Jose can have positive leverage if Ricardo tells him, "I want to buy your car—I love the color." Jose can have negative leverage if Ricardo threatens Jose by saying, "If you don't give me a discount like you promised, I will ruin your reputation."

The amount of buyer leverage relative to the bargaining power and leverage of the seller depends on the perception, information, and insights that the seller and buyer have about the relative scarcity or abundance of the product from the perspective of the other. The relative leverage of either Ricardo as a buyer or Jose as a seller determines the price and terms of transactions and the nature of their negotiation relationships. Business procurement negotiators, for example, use their past purchase histories to get better deals from sellers.

Positive and negative leverage can be balanced using third-party standards and norms to support the value of the buyer or seller. For example, in the car sale, the parties can use a Blue Book value to define or maximize their negotiation leverage.

Leverage for Quantum Negotiators relates to how relatively easy it is for each of the negotiators to walk away. If it is easier for Ricardo to find another car than it is for Jose to find another buyer, Ricardo has stronger leverage. In the end leverage is having something the other guy wants. Or, better yet, needs. Or, best of all, simply cannot do without.

In the Quantum Negotiation mindset, leverage creates more resources and opportunities. Quantum Negotiators evaluate their own and a counterpart's initial leverage by researching how relative the needs and wants are between them, as well as by researching the drivers of decisions. A disciplined evaluation of leverage goes beyond research about what the parties want and need but also how much they want and need it. This information is difficult to assess and is often reluctantly shared; however, the earlier that Quantum Negotiators find out the "how much," the less likely their counterpart will be able to misdirect them about it later.

Leverage is only strong or weak in comparison to the interdependence of needs. In leverage terms, a Quantum Negotiator's needs and wants do not mean much independently. They only gain relevance when analyzed relative to the others parties' needs and wants. For example, if Ricardo as the buyer has limited time relative to Jose, the seller, Jose has positive leverage. Ricardo may state he is desperate to buy because of a limited time frame, even though Jose does not state that he also needs to sell quickly. Relative leverage shifts in the favor of Jose based on the perceptions disclosed in the negotiation. If Ricardo really wants the car, and does not know that Jose is also in a hurry, then Jose has stronger leverage. The perception of the negotiators' needs, not their "true" level of desperation, has an impact on the negotiation.

In addition to the parties' relative levels of need, Quantum Negotiation leverage also depends on what will happen to each party if they cannot reach an agreement. A strong Plan B or BATNA (Best Alternative to a Negotiated Agreement) increases leverage. A weak Plan B means weaker leverage. This leverage is also a relative term. Ricardo's leverage is dependent on other attractive cars to purchase in relation to Jose's potential credible buyers for the car. If both Ricardo and Jose have limited options, they have balanced leverage between them.

Leverage is not always a function of rationality. The factors of trust, respect, "liking," gut feeling, affinity, and so on can play an important role here as well. If you can speak to what is important to the other party and create a sense of "I see you beyond your surface manifestation," you are creating leverage. When people feel seen and understood more deeply, you're setting in motion a gravitational force.

In many ways the tradition in negotiation is to think of a leverage equation. In a linear, Newtonian world you have a finite resource, let's say 100, so it could be split 80/20 or 50/50, but in a quantum definition, there are infinite possibilities of how much leverage and opportunities there are in a negotiation.

Prepare the WHAT of Negotiation—Expanding the ZOPA

A goal in classic negotiation is to win as much ZOPA (Zone of Potential Agreement) as you possibly can. Quantum Negotiators know that seizing value within the ZOPA is more than a contest of wills. Because Quantum Leaders do not believe that we live in a zero-sum world of limited resources, they have a goal to create and expand as much value as possible within the ZOPA with a counterpart.

For example, if negotiator A wants to lend money at a certain interest rate, say 20 percent, over a certain period of time and negotiator B wants to borrow money at 10 percent, the ZOPA is 10 percent on the lower end and 20 percent on the higher end.

Rather than a contest of wills regarding the settlement point, the negotiators can enhance the process of exchange with problem solving and dialogue. Through dialogue about the nature of the relationship, risk sharing, and problem solving, Quantum Leaders can expand the quality of the opportunities within the ZOPA. Sometimes the ZOPA is set around price points, but with a widened perspective negotiators often see that there are many other tangible and intangible needs that can be addressed in order to reach an agreement.

Quantum Negotiators do not rely on classic hardball tactics of negotiation to "lowball" or "highball" opening offers to weaken their counterpart in a negotiation. Instead, they adopt a Quantum Negotiation approach by exploring what they WANT as negotiators and WHY they want it. This helps them clarify their goals, but also enables them to best communicate those goals to their counterparts. They have discovered that part of what they need in a negotiation is a quality relationship with their counterparts.

Practicing the ZOPA

Quantum Negotiators think about how they can encourage more information sharing and problem solving to increase the ZOPA. Quantum Leaders evaluate the range of interests the negotiators have about the future, in both the short and long term. They determine the factors that contribute to the interests of the parties. They assess the levels of the parties' risk tolerance, walk-away point, and willingness to share information and explore options. As they prepare, they evaluate their terms and time preferences before they set the ZOPA. They decide to set a time limit for their negotiation. And finally, they think strategically about how to set and to respond to the first anchor in a negotiation.

Wendy Asks:

I feel a little vulnerable if I communicate to my counterpart about who we are and why we need certain outcomes. Why can't I just state what it is we want and get it?

Anchoring the Potential

Clarity about WHO they are and WHY they need certain outcomes of their negotiation helps Quantum Negotiators prepare to be more confident in WHAT they want in a negotiation. This starts with their parameters used to establish the boundary points within the ZOPA. Setting these boundaries is used by Quantum Negotiators who have experienced the ineffectiveness of lowball/highball tactics and prefer not to use aggressive tactics.

Anchoring the potential boundaries in a negotiation continues the discussion of getting what one wants and can prevent the negotiation from turning from a problem-solving experience into a battle. Anchoring is a critical Quantum Negotiation skill and a core competency for claiming as much as one can from the ZOPA. Proper planning for a problem-solving negotiation helps negotiators to assess the general range of value, that is, which points of contention are more important than others, for their topics of discussion. Such preparation also provides the framework necessary to recognize aggressive initial offers. One needs to know when to insist that a coercive negotiator start again with a reasonable opening offer.

A negotiator who has supporting evidence of market value has a clear alternative to an unreasonable offer and can respond effectively. With proper preparation, a negotiator does not need to yield to an unreasonable offer nor respond with an extreme counteroffer.

Systematic preparation can strengthen a negotiator's skills when they are employing Quantum Negotiation. Exploring the emotional and social underpinnings of loss aversion can give one an edge in the negotiation. A leader's strong impulse to avoid losses is often stronger than the drive to acquire gains. Understanding loss aversion helps a negotiator to frame the initial offer, or the anchor, in a way that mitigates loss to the counterpart, who will then be more likely to cooperate rather than compete in the negotiation. Preventing loss can be a more powerful influence than positioning the anchor as a gain. Preparation is required to present or frame what is wanted. Anchors set the stage for engaging the other party in problem solving instead of battling within the ZOPA.

Francisca's Quantum ZOPA

Francisca, a mechanical services and equipment saleswoman, recently applied this concept in a negotiation. She had a habit of first waiting to hear what a counterpart's initial anchor would be. Francisca would then raise or lower her own opening offer based on that anchor. Later, she learned that the initial offer by the other party was often based on a lack of research about the value of those offers in the marketplace. Francisca saw that the anchors set by the other parties, realistic or not, were treated as benchmarks from which all counterproposals would be made.

During her negotiation studies, Francisca became interested in research on the perception of loss aversion. It is not the reality of loss that matters but the perception of losing something. Even if the net price were the same, would your counterpart rather avoid a $500 surcharge or receive a $500 discount? Be mindful that the same change in price framed differently can have a significant effect on negotiation behavior.

She also became more assertive in setting the first anchor point herself rather than reacting to a counterpart's initial offer. She became increasingly aware of how often anchor points are set carelessly and unrealistically in negotiations.

Francisca utilized Quantum Negotiation by encouraging her counterparts to expand their notion of the ZOPA's fixed resources and opportunities. In doing so, she afforded herself a more precise and comfortable ZOPA range.

Quantum Negotiation for WHAT Mark Needs

Mark, an account executive, once believed that the best way to start a negotiation was with pressure and an extreme position. His idea was that negotiators should let others know who's in charge by taking a hard line.

Mark later began to wonder whether a negotiator could soften his position if need be. He noticed that the more extreme his opening position, and the smaller the concessions, the more time and effort it took to reach an agreement. Mark could see that when each side tried to use force to make the other change its position, anger and resentment resulted. This tension put a strain on his relationships with his customers.

One of the negotiation goals Mark set for himself was to encourage his clients to develop and to yield to objective criteria and for all parties to stop using pressure tactics against one another. He believed that it had been a mistake to use threats and aggressive tactics with his clients rather than Quantum Negotiation to influence them.

In addition to having a good alternative for negotiations with his customers, Mark researched a list of specific market trends, industry precedents, and competitors' standards on which he could base his initial offers. He found that this allowed him to make a clear and firm first offer.

When Mark researched industry standards and the competitors with whom his customers had a history, he was able to align himself with his customers' values. He found that his interactions with customers were more successful when they worked jointly to discuss and design objective criteria and standards of legitimacy they could agree on. It became easier to shape proposals and to find solutions with his customers in this new environment.

The use of objective criteria is a great way to increase a negotiator's power, authority, legitimacy, and fairness. In this way, Quantum Negotiators find ways to seek power with clients, as opposed to power over them. When qualified research on third-party standards are employed, such as market trends, industry precedents, or price benchmarks, the parties can yield to these fair standards. By harnessing third-party standards, negotiators can focus on fair and objective principles to depersonalize their tactics. In this way, they remove the tension of coercive power and aggression in the process.

The more objective and independent the standard is, the less overt and destructive emotions will be in a negotiation. Objective criteria can also provide a good-faith basis for offers and anchors, concessions, and inclinations for more collaboration and sharing.

Losing the Ability to Influence What We WANT

Eight years ago, Geetha took a director position at a software company with flexible working hours. She could determine her own work schedule and meeting times within a small, energized global organization. The office atmosphere was casual, hours were determined by clients' situations, and calls were often arranged within days or hours of requests. She loved her job and was rewarded as a valued, inclusive leader.

However, after Geetha received her promotion, her company was acquired by an ambitious "digital 2.0" company hoping to make the exponential leap all the way to a "digital 4.0" one. She was retained while many of her colleagues were laid off. Despite the disappointment of losing some of her best employees, she was excited to influence the direction of the new expanding enterprise.

Within a few months, Geetha became extremely tired and even depressed about her ability to engage with her new colleagues. Geetha became very anxious about having to bend her family life and clients' odd working hours around a new standard workweek rule. She was aware that her leadership influence and visibility would require working within the standardized rules, regulations, and policies. Geetha knew the transformation would be difficult, but she didn't think it would affect her so dramatically.

In a Quantum Negotiation coaching session, Geetha explored why she lost her ability to influence what she wanted from her previous management or her new one. For most of her career, Geetha had been an energized and capable negotiator, problem solver, and facilitator. She was surprised to find that she had become very aggressive, short-tempered, and controlling whenever she met with her team or clients. She wasn't getting anything done, and she felt harsh resistance from others as she tried to push an agenda. It was exhausting.

Upon review of her Quantum Negotiation Profile she discovered that she had an unconscious prejudice about rules in general. She valued loyalty to her family and social network, and above all, loose rules about work time. Upon reflection, she realized that all her adult life she had been rewarded for her flexibility and creativity to work around the rules in both her career and family life. This was no longer rewarded, and thus she had become unanchored and adrift.

As part of her coaching session homework, she became more observant of the value her new colleagues placed on universal rules and procedures because this created a sense of fairness and consistency. Upon exploring the mindset of her new partners, she came to appreciate how they prided themselves on impartial laws, principles, and equal rights as their brand image. She began to see how her preference for favoritism and freewheeling rules was inefficient for a growing enterprise with new opportunities. She also realized that her lack of consistency about her work schedule was more time-consuming than it needed to be.

With Geetha's new appreciation for the value of standard rules and rights, she could understand why she was losing her leadership edge. With this new motivation, she realized that she was behaving in a disrespectful and obstructionist way. Rather than complain and debate the way she wanted things to be, she practiced speaking more optimistically about the benefits of the standard policies announced each day. Another part of Geetha's coaching homework was to organize a more standardized time frame to speak with clients, for example. With practice, and by expressing optimism with colleagues and clients, she became more comfortable and engaged in the expanding global initiatives.

Now, Geetha loves her new job as the vice president of global operations despite the disruption in her career path posed by the acquisition. Her leadership and personal development required not only that she add more skills, but also that she "let go" of or unlearn habits and assumptions that had been successful in the past.

Geetha noticed WHAT she wanted was more important than sticking with her habitual way of getting it. She learned to style-shift and plan for how she could encourage others to help her reach all her goals.

WHAT IF—*You Don't Reach an Agreement: Mapping and Evaluation*

Quantum Leaders find it useful to explore their leverage by mapping out the need levels for themselves and their counterpart. Mapping and evaluation enhances their ability to negotiate strategically, especially if they cannot reach an agreement. WHAT IF they reach an impasse, or the agreement is too imbalanced against them? They go to their Plan B.

Quantum Negotiators improve their alternatives to a negotiation before the process begins. This increases their options for problem solving. This is the Best Alternative to a Negotiated Agreement, or BATNA, as outlined by the classic *Getting to Yes* by Roger Fisher and William Ury. Knowing the potential alternatives is crucial to the outcome of the negotiation. Whether it concludes in agreement or walking away, Quantum Leaders map out alternatives. With an alternative or Plan B to a negotiation, they can increase their options when dealing with someone who may undermine their goals.

It is also important for Quantum Leaders to determine authority in the negotiation: profile the other party's history, reputation, and tactics. When they do this they often maximize their ability to walk away from a bad negotiation or uncooperative counterpart.

Analyze Fair and Objective Criteria

Quantum Negotiation continues to explore what the parties want in a negotiation by focusing on how to use mutually relevant criteria, rather than a battle of wills, to increase their power in a negotiation. This framework also addresses how the practices of independent, fair, and objective standards can be used to change the interaction from a coercive negotiation to one of understanding and problem solving. The preparation for this problem-solving approach involves research on which fair standards can be used in the negotiation in place of manipulation tactics.

Quantum Negotiation builds on the notion that negotiation is a process of communication in which the parties aim to influence each other's perceptions, attitudes, and even intentions. Quantum Negotiation increases the negotiator's ability to encourage a counterpart to cooperate in problem solving.

It is critical to analyze fair and unbiased criteria of standards and procedures that can drive an objective and independent process for negotiation. When Quantum Leaders and their counterparts can yield to a market or industry precedent, a professional standard, a third-party opinion, a traditional procedure, or an efficiency standard, the negotiation can be a problem-solving experience rather than a contest of wills. If both sides can agree on an independent standard rule, for example, or a process that is fair and satisfying, it is more likely that the conclusion will be a sustainable outcome. If not, reaching agreement is likely to be far more difficult and contentious.

Quantum Plan B for Narcissist Tactics

Narcissism is an exaggerated egoistic tendency often associated with coercive negotiators. It is often difficult for Quantum Negotiators to respond to negotiators who demonstrate narcissistic traits and place themselves at the center of the negotiation with no concern for others. Quantum Leaders can identify narcissistic tactics and ways that coercive counterparts can undermine a mutual-gains and balanced strategy.

Wendy Asks:

How do you identify a narcissist? I am sure that I have worked with some, but I am curious of how you know it is no longer worth negotiating.

Patience can enable Quantum Negotiators to keep a client whom others might drop. Forbearance is the ability to look past a coercive negotiator's boorishness, selfishness, and arrogance when you see the potential for a valuable agreement. However, if your needs cannot be met in a coercive negotiation situation, Quantum Negotiators say the best course is to end the negotiations. Calculate the sense of satisfaction that you will have if you continue the negotiation compared with alternative negotiation partners or clients. When the losses are too extreme for you, end the negotiation and turn to your alternative plan.

Quantum Preparation Summary

Quantum Leaders know WHO they are on multiple levels: the way they think, feel, believe, behave, and perform. They also know WHAT they want, WHY they want it, and their WHAT IF alternatives should the negotiation not give them what they need.

When negotiators evaluate what purpose and significance a negotiation has for them, they also consider how their goals can be achieved by better aligning with the beliefs of their counterpart. These negotiators can recognize their own potentially destructive negotiation habits. This deeper understanding of WHO they are and WHY their counterpart shares a sense of purpose helps both parties to transcend many of the limitations often found in negotiation.

Most negotiators prepare WHAT their own targets, limits, anchors, and alternatives are before negotiation. However, there is a distinction between those who prepare not only WHAT they need, but also WHAT their counterpart needs—that is, where there are common interests.

Often a critical difference among great negotiators relative to mediocre ones is the ability to expand the zone of potential agreements by understanding the range of shared needs with a counterpart. Jointly engaging in and widening the potential of numerous options and resources creates more opportunities and solutions for all parties.

WHAT IF there is a possibility that a negotiation reaches impasse or breakdown? The distinction between a successful and a mediocre negotiator is that there is an exploration of not only one's own alternative or Plan B to the negotiation, but also an exploration of what options their counterpart may have (or not have) if no agreement is possible.

In our next chapter we'll explore more about HOW Quantum Negotiators approach their negotiations.

Quantum Leaders have clarity about WHO, WHAT, WHY, WHAT IF, and HOW. They explore what their ZOPA is and how their counterpart may behave in context of their own history, cultural perspective, and expectations of the negotiation process have greater impact on reaching their goals. If there are gaps in behaviors or styles of negotiating between the negotiators, Quantum Leaders will prepare to style-shift, for example, to encourage more engaging behaviors with their counterpart.

In that sense, Quantum Negotiations are distinguished by their inclusive mindset, attitude, and skillset. They are aware that when at least one of the negotiators is willing to explore another's perceptions and preferred negotiation experience, then they can unlock many new opportunities and potential for all parties.

3

The HOW of Quantum Negotiation

After the death of their father, two brothers and a sister were about to inherit equal shares of a family cabin in Montana. In the first meeting about their father's estate settlement, the middle brother, John, said he wanted to purchase his younger brother Ben's one-third ownership, making John two-thirds owner and his older sister, Amy, a one-third owner.

Ben said he could offer to sell his one-third equally to John and Amy. However, John pointed out to them that he was the only one with the financial resources to buy it. In addition, John and his grown children lived in Montana within driving distance of the cabin. John's work responsibilities made it difficult to plan in advance to use the cabin and he wanted the freedom to meet his children and friends there on short notice. Amy and her family lived on the East Coast and would only visit on holidays.

Amy could only pay one-third of the property taxes and upkeep, which would be managed by John, and she expected use of the cabin one-third of the time. Adding to the tension over scheduling, John also said he wanted to renovate and "update" the cabin, which would be expensive because of mountain zoning and building restrictions.

Amy thought a remodel was not necessary and would not pay for John's remodeling ideas—which she thought were ridiculous. After the first contentious estate meeting, Amy went with her sons to the cabin the next weekend, knowing no one was there, and took all the Navajo rugs, pots, and Western art. Her fear was that they would be "tossed" in a possible remodel. This incensed John. The tension between Amy and John over the details led to a crescendo of "very mean" things said to each other. It was like they were children again.

Ben soon learned of the arguing and "thievery" and became alarmed that not only would their father's estate settlement go on for years and cost thousands of dollars, but even more important, that their family would forever be divided by this.

★ ★ ★

Quantum Leadership—HOW to Negotiate

No one wants to get taken advantage of in a negotiation. Because of that fear, many negotiators believe they need to start with an aggressive or deceptive strategy in order to protect themselves. Ultimately this doesn't get them what they need.

Quantum Negotiation leverages behavior and strategy that motivates counterparts to share tangible and intangible needs. Quality information sparks effective dialogue and problem-solving processes. This approach is called an integrative or mutual-gains strategy. The strategy integrates your interests, goals, and needs along with those of your counterpart. It does not employ the primal stress and tricks of CC&D—concealment, camouflage, and deception.

Buoyancy is achieved through integration of the five human dimensions (cognitive, emotional, social, physical, and spiritual). This integrated and balanced approach brings clarity and creativity to situations of uncertainty, fear, and complexity. This power is like an integrated circuit board that combines individual semiconductor devices and bonds them into one powerful unit—just like an anchor to a buoy in a hurricane.

Quantum Negotiators prepare and design strategies focused on all the human dimensions as they align their vitality and stamina, leading others to do the same. Skilled negotiators increase the chances of accomplishing their goals through clarity and buoyancy rather than through CC&D preparation. Even in the midst of a coercive negotiation process, it is possible to reevaluate preparation and strategy to be in alignment with one's personal beliefs and in balance with the other dimensions of one's life.

Using the Whole Brain

Findings about emotional and social intelligence conclude that negotiators can increase the power to influence not for manipulation, but for more productive facilitation practices. Increasingly, Quantum Leaders require vital facilitation skills that foster sustainable agreements that meet not only their own objectives, but also satisfy others' desires. A disciplined understanding of how our human brain processes not only helps with clear strategic information, but also with the emotional elements that yield more constructive and satisfying negotiation relationships and solutions.

Quantum Leaders have a facilitation talent that is accomplished through what social neuroscientists say is leveraging the system of the brain's interconnectedness and coordination of its left and right hemispheres. For example, when interpersonal competencies are built on specific neural circuits and related endocrine systems that inspire others to be effective and cooperative, the power to constructively influence others is increased. It may appear quite simple to coordinate left and right brain functions, but it requires disciplined attention, nurturance, and practice.

It has become evident in the last decade that the basic research in neuroscience can now be understood and applied in such real-life situations as negotiation. This may seem pretty esoteric at first; however, it continues to be proven both in laboratory settings and in boardrooms.

One of the fundamental scientific discoveries is that the utilization of our whole brain can be a powerful tool in problem solving, especially in complex and ambiguous situations. For example, neither intricate personal nor critical contract negotiations can be managed alone with logical, linear, and computer-like thinking. Such negotiations also require key skills of self-knowledge, empathy, and detection of human interaction subtleties.

By embracing the functions of both the left and right hemispheres of the brain, Quantum Leaders find that this can provide considerable guidance for not only their personal lives, but also their professional negotiation endeavors.

The left hemisphere activities of analysis, rationality, and logical planning enhanced with right hemisphere competencies of interpreting emotions and recognition of nonverbal expressions increase a Quantum Negotiator's power to facilitate mutual-gains outcomes. Successful leaders conclude that not only do negotiators need to prepare in a logical and sequential way to communicate to and be understood by others, but they also need to think simultaneously about what is not verbally communicated.

Because about only 7 percent of communication is verbal and understood by the analytical left side of our brains, Quantum Negotiators need to read the rest nonverbally! Research shows us that body language (38 percent) and facial expressions (55 percent) are read by the right side of our brains. This nonverbal communication requires a right-brain skill to read what is often unsaid (which is a very prominent aspect of cross-cultural negotiation). If nonverbal messages and the emotional cues sent via speech patterns, facial expressions, and body posture are not adequately read by a negotiator, agreements are almost impossible to accomplish.

In addition to these findings, research suggests that adversarial contention constricts the possibility for the left and right hemispheres of the brain to work together; thus confirming that buoyant and sociocentric negotiation strategies are more· effective than the conventional approaches. It's very hard to take an adversarial position and then switch to a collaborative approach later on.

The skill development of both the right and left hemisphere of our brains is essential for Quantum Negotiation planning, which analyzes: (1) the details and strategies (left), and (2) the synthesis of the big picture and relationships (right). Both are essential to human reasoning, social interactions, and successful negotiation processes.

The biological underpinning called brain neural links are the connections between neurons in the brain that form neural circuits and networks that generate our perceptions of the world and our behavior. These connections in our brain occur when negotiators consciously or unconsciously detect and attune themselves to someone else's emotions in a negotiation. This social and emotional intelligence is a powerful way to leverage the brain's interconnectedness. The mastery of fostering positive emotions of cooperation and support are fundamentally necessary to accomplish complex negotiation needs.

Quantum Negotiation explores reframing leadership and negotiation in the context of interdependence and relationships. Quantum Leaders orient themselves as leaders in the context of relationships, the team, or the organization when developing strategies and tactics as a negotiator. A Quantum Leader mindfully responds to others and the relationship rather than reacting to the primal stress of fear with manipulation.

Quantum Divorce Negotiation

Alexandra (she goes by "Alex"), is a lawyer and a well-trained and practiced negotiator in both her professional and personal life. During a coercive personal negotiation with her ex-husband, Alex reached the limits of what she was sacrificing during negotiation: specifically, her physical and emotional health.

Alex felt as though she had been in battle. She needed to leave the battlefield and regroup. After assessing her own values and previous strategies, she made a conscious choice to remain aware of herself. She began to explore her emotional, social, and spiritual values as a negotiator. As she became more anchored with all the values and dimensions in her life, she "unfroze" from her self-defensive attitude and realized that her ex-husband lacked the awareness and skills for collaboration. This process enabled Alex to make a transition from coercive negotiation to Quantum Negotiation and unleash her stamina and vitality as a negotiator.

Alex's heightened consciousness helped her to rethink how she negotiated. As she balanced, anchored, and became buoyant she was enabled to apply the Quantum Negotiation principles even against a coercive adversary like her ex-husband. She was able to do this through five simple steps:

1. Prepare
2. Clarify her dimensions for herself
3. Ask about her counterpart's needs
4. Express her needs clearly
5. Work with her counterpart, not against

Now when Alex feels preyed upon while negotiating, she makes time for resting, retreating, being more playful and creative, and maintaining a curious attitude about herself and her counterpart. She is in awe of how her spiritual connection to a higher purpose has translated into an ability to connect with others. This provides a new source of energy, physical power, strength, and stamina for Alex and is an effective way of dealing with her frequent bouts of fatigue, which manipulative negotiators may use against her.

Her clarity about her emotions makes it possible for her to set the stage by being the first to express respect. A sense of satisfaction in a negotiation comes when she can model the understanding behaviors that she would like to receive.

Like Alex, Quantum Negotiators increase the chances of accomplishing their goals through anchoring and clarity more so than by concealment, camouflage, and deception. By anchoring and balancing their human needs, they become more adaptable and creative even in a situation of coercive power. Preparation and reflection help them to accomplish desired goals by bringing an increased ability for behaving in satisfying and successful ways.

HOW to Behave as a Quantum Negotiator

Quantum Negotiators explore a strategic design that will increase social engagement and sharing of critical information in negotiation. Leaders must have a strategy to meet fundamental demands of durability, utility, and satisfaction. The high costs of relationships and the economic/social stresses of coercive strategies require practical steps for Quantum Leaders. This requires them to negotiate in a way that increases cooperation and risk sharing. An appropriate strategy is an important part of a focused negotiation process. In the majority of cases where you will negotiate to get what you need from others, it is better to spend your energy planning rather than focusing on tactics.

A key part of this strategy is influencing the setting; or, in other words, creating the context for yourself and for others to show up in a way that is most conducive to the outcome you are looking for.

Thomas Asks:

What are some of the practices that you can adopt to create an environment that is more conducive to collaboration and building trust?

1. Approach the negotiation with the right attitude. If you feel very competitive, or have a desire to coerce your counterpart, then you're not ready for a negotiation.
2. Approach the negotiation with an openness to explore the options or perspectives of your counterpart.
   a. People tend to assume you are thinking only of yourself in a negotiation. It is counterintuitive for them to hear that you'd like to understand their perspective. If the other person feels included in the sharing of perspectives, then you're taking opposition away and encouraging collaboration.
3. Create the meta-negotiation—how will you negotiate with each other? Be transparent about your intentions. Come to an agreement on how you will treat each other. Reaffirm your shared purpose for negotiating together.
4. Extend yourself to listen, be more curious, and understand the problem from your counterpart's point of view to build trust.
5. Talk from the "we" rather than the I. Talk from a shared interest in resolving something and make the substance of the negation the thing that needs to be resolved and addressed.

We also must be aware of how we go about our communication during negotiation. There are several frequencies at which we send information to others:

- The first level is the subject matter: What are we talking about?
- The second level is our frame of reference, value system, and how we are viewing something.
- The third level is our identity—who we are, how we are seen, and what defines us.
- The fourth level is emotion—do we feel a sense of bonding with our counterpart?

On all four of these levels we need to create a relationship with our counterparts. On the first three levels we need to recognize that we may operate on different premises, and seek to understand one another. But on the fourth level, we need to think about whether our behaviors are connecting us or driving us apart.

It has to be authentic; otherwise it won't work. If you're professing to be very collaborative and then the other person sees that as a kind of a tactic that you're hiding, that erodes trust. The biggest principle in trust is being fairly authentic and articulate about what is going on, not only verbally, but also nonverbally. The research in neuroscience shows that inauthenticity at the neurological level can be read nonverbally. No matter what words you say, your authenticity is being read on a subconscious level.

Very often in the conventional rational approach to negotiation, we don't want to allow intuition to have a role—but Quantum Negotiators understand the importance of paying attention to what they are feeling.

> ## Thomas Asks:
>
> How can I establish rapport with my counterpart without falling into the trap of being overly accommodating and sacrificing my own needs?

Developing a Sociocentric Orientation

A Quantum Negotiator plans to offer solutions to a counterpart because they first identify their compatible interests and the potential for mutual gains by reorienting from an egocentric point of view to a sociocentric point of view. A sociocentric orientation of self-interest provides the mutuality and insight necessary to guide the negotiation dialogue by engaging, listening, and keeping in mind the interests of both parties. A Quantum Leader does not abandon one's own goals for the sake of others, as an altruist might. A sociocentric orientation helps negotiators realistically acknowledge that their own and their counterpart's self-interests are connected and related to each other.

In negotiation, accepting and listening to your counterparts can motivate them to be more trusting and cooperative in solving problems. An anxious or controlling negotiator is unlikely to recognize that the self-interests of the parties are in fact compatible. A Quantum Leader guides the parties to recognize when self-interests are aligned. Each party can then be recognized as autonomous, but still interconnected, in decision making.

Quantum Negotiators explore who they are as negotiators in the context of their social conditioning. They explore all of their human dimensions—cognitive, psychological, social, physical, and spiritual.

Quantum Negotiators have a strong sense of self and identity, and are anchored to their own values. They have the curiosity, the resilience, and the intelligence to understand another's point of view and interests. This requires a meta-negotiation—a negotiation about how we will negotiate and what norms we can create together before we negotiate.

HOW to Behave as a Negotiator—Mexican-Russian Relations

Federico, from Mexico, engaged in a negotiation with a Russian coworker, Uri, who was a difficult person to deal with. They co-led a project centralizing their organization's digital and information technology system. Federico and Uri had to negotiate the basic elements of the project design together. Federico and Uri each had cultural preferences that generally aligned with the national style orientations of Mexico and Russia, respectively. However, Federico did not believe cultural differences would have much impact on team interactions, as they were both engineers and spoke the same technical language.

Federico's cultural preference was to be indirect in his communication, while Uri's was very direct. Federico was reacting unconsciously to Uri's direct communication. Federico thought that Uri's direct style meant that he did not want to cooperate.

After several days of getting nowhere, Federico realized that he had been using a coercive negotiation strategy, trying to exercise his power over his coworker. Up until that point, Federico had been obsessed with their differences concerning the subject of the negotiation. Federico could see that his coercive negotiation strategy with Uri was counterproductive. Federico began to behave more like a Quantum Negotiator and began to focus on commonalities rather than the differences that arose between them on issues.

Federico reset the preliminary phase of the negotiation by establishing a positive relationship between him and Uri. He began the next meeting by expressing optimism about the outcome, pointing out areas of agreement and common interests that had already been discussed. He then asked Uri what other issues or agenda items he would like to discuss before they made any decisions. Federico made a list of questions for Uri, encouraging him to see the two of them as partners.

Once they were asking and answering questions of one another, Federico suggested an opening phase where they could state their positions and propose possible solutions. They would listen to one another and then summarize their conflicts and areas of disagreement. Federico ensured their issues were acknowledged after the proposals were made. When Federico became more conscious of his Quantum Negotiation strategy, he could construct and lead a negotiation that increased cooperation and information sharing. He was amazed at how well they both were able to address their needs and interests in a noncoercive way.

With a better relationship and more insight about their common and conflicting issues, Uri and Federico began an exploration phase, searching for final design options. Federico listened and did not reject Uri's suggestions. Instead, he asked more questions as Uri shared a solution, but did not defend his own priorities.

Federico found that this exploring phase was the most engaging aspect of the negotiation. He became energized and excited when they discussed how each of them could meet his own budget and scheduling needs. Instead of defensively holding to one idea, they spent time exploring why different solutions could or could not be implemented, without any attachment to a particular solution. Federico also learned that Uri's direct communication style did not necessarily mean he was coercive, but that he liked to ask and answer questions in a direct way.

Finally, Federico knew that they had reached the closing. He planned to evaluate how reasonable their offers and trades were. Where they still saw some difficulties in getting the project done by the deadline they had chosen, they problem-solved together, finding a way to overcome the difficulties. Federico made it clear to Uri that they both would have to develop action plans and follow up on various issues before the work began. As part of the closing stage of the negotiation, they discussed how the project would benefit each of them personally as well as the company.

When Federico shifted from a positional, aggressive approach, he found that there was a better exchange of information and ideas. He was surprised at how many options they had invented for the project as a result.

The design plan that Federico and Uri employed stimulated innovation in negotiations. Curiosity and engagement on opposing and diverse points of view led to breakthrough thinking. When Quantum Negotiators can create a climate of collaboration and inclusion, they can encourage others, seek support, and lead an effective analytic and problem-solving process. Quantum Leaders, like Federico, use the critical skills of awareness, including self-awareness, feedback, self-disclosure, problem identification, listening, and empathy.

Wendy Asks:

Do you ever think that it's a good idea to use deception or to camouflage your needs, interest, or behavior in a negotiation? In all of your experiences, do you ever feel there is a need to prepare for that?

In the majority of cases, this strategy will be counterproductive to the outcome of the negotiation, especially if the relationship is critical to actually execute the agreement you've made with each other. It's pretty risky—it could undermine the working or personal relationship.

There are perhaps two situations where bluffing is not negative:

The first situation is in a purely transactional negotiation. For example, let's say you buy some trinket at the market when you are on vacation. There is nothing at stake other than you buying that trinket at the lowest price. In this case, you may just bluff about what you are willing to pay.

The second situation is in the intercultural space, where there are cultural norms and expectations around bargaining patterns. For example, in Japan you would set a very narrow bargaining range. You would be seen as extremely deceptive, or unprepared, or stupid if you had a really wide bargaining range. But if you go to Mexico for example, on the street you would set at least a 30 percent higher bargaining range, because that's just a part of the game. In these cases, you are style-shifting to adapt to the cultural norms.

Wendy Asks:

So when is it authentic and when is it just part of a manipulation strategy?

You can't really tell from the outside. It's all about intention. If your intention is to establish trust, and that's your true and authentic intention, then you filter it through the social context and language that someone else understands.

The back-and-forth of a negotiation are also good signs that it is authentic. Are they giving you feedback to actually know that their problems are getting solved? Is your intention actually being perceived as one that is going to help them solve their issue? If the other party doesn't sense that they are really getting their proposals accepted or their problems aren't being solved, you will know it in their behavior.

★ ★ ★

Designing a Quantum Plan to Win

Rather than focusing on egoistic, competitive, coercive winning over a counterpart, a Quantum Negotiation has a wider set of variables for success. Quantum Negotiators know the coercive model is not in sync with the social and economic realities of the contemporary marketplace and sustainable relationships. Even though Quantum Negotiators recognize the value of mutual-gains negotiation strategy, they must develop mindfulness about their own habits of classic coercive power, because they can often be difficult to overcome.

A mindful and disciplined plan for Quantum Negotiation yields significant creative and sustainable benefits and opportunities. Quantum Negotiation success is not only measured by tangible wealth alone (e.g., land, financial capital, and assets), but also by assessments of intangible fortunes (e.g., social and emotional capital, increased sense of purpose and satisfaction).

Cecile's Reward

Cecile had received her highest financial bonus ever that summer, but didn't feel any satisfaction with this reward. She had done very well in a consulting firm, and was well compensated as a result, but she had had little time to reflect on her experiences and her value system. It was not that she wanted greater financial success; it was something more that was missing. She took the months of unused vacation time that she had accumulated to deal with this void in her emotional health.

Cecile felt that she needed to slow down and understand why she had moved professionally so far from her desire for a meaningful career. Cecile, like many other experienced negotiators, wanted to achieve a standard of living and success that included both material and intangible assets.

Upon reflection, Cecile realized that she had gotten out of control. She had unknowingly defaulted to classic notions about power in her interactions with clients and coworkers. As she gained significant financial rewards, she became increasingly aware of her isolation from professional and social connections. In her professional life, she wasn't helping others as she had wanted to do.

Cecile had not realized how stressful it was to struggle for survival as she protected her status and position. She noticed that alliances and networks were developing in her business unit without her. Other teams of consultants were able to keep all their client contracts over several years, but she was losing many clients over the years. She valued relationships and wanted to provide service to others. She wanted to integrate her professional experiences into the broader canvas of her life.

By the time autumn arrived, Cecile had developed a Quantum Negotiation mindset and skillset, helping her to recover a sense of purpose and willingness for problem solving with others. She realized that she had lost power as she became scattered and out of alignment with her own cognitive, emotional, social, physical, and spiritual needs. As Cecile became more mindful of the problem-solving mental model of power, she was able to gain energy from all the human dimensions.

Her breakthrough thinking was difficult, but not impossible. Now, Cecile enjoys the financial aspects of her career, as well as a sense of satisfaction and an integration of her personal and professional needs.

Quantum Leadership Transforms Organizational "Silo" Behavior

In addition to individual Quantum Leaders who want to gain negotiation proficiency, organizations also struggle with managing the disparate parts within an institution. Organizations need information management systems for supporting a Quantum Negotiation strategy on which individual negotiators can rely. The strategy must include organizational commitment, clarity, flexibility, and leverage. Quantum organizations are now designing better preparation techniques and providing ongoing support and assistance. They see negotiation as an organizational capability designed around a sound mutual-gains approach.

Quantum Leaders redefine power, and organizations can enhance performance by grounding their institutional strategy in relevant Quantum Negotiation practices of systematic preparation. The mutual gains for individuals and organizations through Quantum Negotiation principles necessitate a preparation involving attention to divergent interests within an organization.

Self-reflection, monitoring, and continuous improvement will become core competencies for individuals and organizations using information management tools and Quantum Negotiation planning and performance systems as ways to reinforce negotiation, learning, and feedback.

Responding to Manipulation Tactics

Thomas Asks:

If somebody does try to manipulate and undermine me with a Machiavellian strategy, what can I do?

Quantum Negotiators lead a mutual-gains approach and maintain a sense of purpose and integrity. Quantum Leaders can identify coercive tactics as they occur. Knowledge about coercive tactics is a source of power for leaders, and provides insight about how to strip away the potency of such tactics.

Quantum Negotiators do not respond in kind with aggressive tactics when they are used against them. They understand how costly such methods are and how often they backfire. Coercive negotiators' manipulation tactics often work because they can shift the confidence and leverage in a negotiation away from you, the target, and toward the manipulator. These tactics can turn you toward revenge or toward an escalation into a nasty and exhausting battle of wills.

In an attempt to establish their power, coercive negotiators may make jokes or sling insults about their counterpart's appearance or ethnicity. In more subtle ways, a manipulator can sabotage a constructive dialogue toward a contest of wills in which the coercive negotiator always wins. For example, if a Quantum Leader wants to discuss an uncomfortable topic, such as a missed deadline, the manipulator will focus on a word or phrase, such as "team success." The coercive negotiator will disagree with how it has been used, and assign a new definition to that word or phrase. They will claim that they know what the project timeline should be for the team, despite an earlier agreement. Many tactics amount to verbal abuse, because a manipulator continues to reject any definition of the words until the counterpart gives up. The manipulator then wins by avoiding the central problems at hand.

Most manipulative negotiation tactics work because accommodating negotiators find it difficult to believe someone could be so cunning, devious, and ruthless. Even if predatory behavior does not take place at the negotiation table, a predator can indirectly undermine a counterpart's confidence and their will to speak. Negotiators who are not prepared often give in when a coercive negotiator makes aggressive claims and preys on their vulnerabilities.

Quantum Negotiators have several options for responding to coercive tactics or predators:

- Ignoring the manipulation tactic: Pretend that you did not hear or see it. You might call a break, switch topics, or ask the manipulator to repeat what has been said.
- Discussing the tactics: Call out and label the action and indicate to the coercive negotiator that you know what's going on and you will not engage in coercive behavior yourself. For example, you could say, "We profess collaboration, but you know, I don't see your behavior as truly collaborative." Give your counterpart options and choices to reciprocate your quantum approach.
- Leading the integrative negotiation: Through dialogue and discussion, stress the importance of the problems and needs you have in common. Return to the meta-negotiation and reaffirm basic principles. Support your counterpart to switch her or his approach and reset.
- Leaving the negotiation or coercive counterpart for an alternative solution—a better job or negotiation partner. You're not desperate to give into something that is abusive. You have other options. A true, clinical narcissist is going to take advantage of you at every move; you

need to be prepared to go to your alternative, and not bleed to death in this situation.

Thomas Asks:

But what if my counterpart has a monopoly?

Consider this—is the monopoly real or perceived? If you think about it, you'll realize that it's really a perception. We usually don't spend time thinking about this because the other party makes it appear that they are more crucial than they really are. They use everything they have to keep us psychologically confined to our dependence on them.

Quantum Negotiators manage aggressive tactics used by coercive parties by guiding the counterpart away from a coercive path and by introducing opportunities to problem solve:

- If a counterpart makes an opening offer that is unrealistic, you can refer to the third-party standards or criteria that you found during your preparation.
- If a counterpart nibbles away at an agreement by asking for small concessions on extraneous points, consider going over the entire package again. Suggestions to dismantle all that has already been negotiated will limit the nibbles.
- If a counterpart begins to make threats or coerce you, review your alternative to negotiating with this counterpart. Also, review and research how strong your counterpart's alternatives are relative to negotiating with you.

How Quantum Negotiators Handle "Hardball" Tactics

Jacques, a real estate agent, represented Roberto, who was selling a luxury condominium. Roberto behaved as a "self-absorbed, demeaning, and demanding" client over a week as they tried to list the property. Roberto had an unreasonable assessment of the comparable market when he positioned his asking price.

Although Jacques had worked with strong-willed clients before, Roberto exhibited traits that Jacques recognized as hardball. In addition, Roberto had a grandiose sense of himself, a need for special consideration for his "unique" condo, and a lack of empathy. Jacques first thought it was just a matter of negotiation style that made it so difficult to engage with Roberto.

However, Jacques soon noticed tactics of deliberate deception, psychological warfare, threats, and coercive behaviors. Jacques became concerned with the way Roberto tried to take advantage of him with extreme demands and very few or small concessions. Jacques continued to be polite, but he would not agree or counteroffer.

Because Jacques had anchored WHAT he needed and WHY, Jacques did not give in to Roberto's attempts to make him flinch. Roberto used "good cop, bad cop" with his wife as the good cop. Jacques was tempted to use his own "bad cop," but did not want to give in to these tactics himself.

Roberto began to make personal insults in ways that could have made Jacques feel vulnerable. However, Jacques observed that when one tactic would not work, Roberto unemotionally moved quickly to others, such as threats and invalidating Jacques' other clients. Despite this, Jacques continued to practice various ways to interact with Roberto. He listened carefully to elicit good information about Roberto's concerns, and gave him positive recognition. Jacques noticed that Roberto had a very low tolerance for frustration so he avoided challenging Roberto's demands.

After all of Jacques' smiles, patience, forbearance, and focus, Roberto still was not realistic about Jacques' commission. At the end of a week of exhausting demands, deceptions, and pressures, Jacques thought about his alternatives to continuing his relationship with Roberto. Jacques concluded that he was dealing with someone who would not engage in a relationship based on negotiation and decided to move on to work with other clients who were selling condos in the same complex.

When Roberto finally played his "take it or leave it" tactic, Jacques named the tactic and said he would "leave it." Jacques terminated the agreement with Roberto, but reflected first on how hostile Roberto would become. However, the price of limiting his own interests and wasting his time to win at this hardball game was not worth it.

Within a week, Jacques began working with two other sellers in the building. They were able to get a good price for their property and he received a fair commission for himself.

Jacques reports that his leadership development in Quantum Negotiation provided him with the confidence to stay anchored in his own values about relationships and to behave in a powerful way to get what he needs in his negotiations.

Wendy Asks:

Are there any practices Quantum Negotiators can use to handle tough situations like the one Jacques experienced, but still engage in business?

Quantum Negotiation and Aikido

In classic notions of power, conflict is considered immutable and inevitable. The word *conflict* is closely associated with a contest. It is assumed in classic theory that those without the required material resources or authority are negotiation losers even before they begin. Those with the structural resources and authority must be disciplined, egoistic, and have a "winner-take-all" orientation to leadership. Leaders who continue to use coercive power plan to mercilessly defeat negotiation opponents in a battle of wills, seeing every conflict as an absolute win-lose contest.

Quantum Leadership Embraces the Opportunities in Conflict and Change

The Quantum approach is much like Aikido, the Japanese martial art that focuses on allowing practitioners to defend themselves while also protecting their attacker from injury. Martial arts principles in general and Aikido practices in particular provide great alternative views for negotiators about the principles and tactics used to share limited resources.

In Aikido, which is translated as a way of blending energy, the practitioner matches the motion of the attacker, redirecting the force of the attack, rather than opposing it head-on. This requires very little physical energy, as the practitioner leads the attacker's momentum using turning movements. The key principle in using these tactics is to align to the rhythm and intent of the attacker to find the optimal position and timing to apply a counter technique.

Many Aikido negotiators interpret these physical tactics as a metaphor for powerful techniques and countertactics when being controlled or attacked in a negotiation situation. The Aikido mindset illustrates how negotiators in conflict situations can avoid assuming the goal of destroying their counterparts and instead block their attacks. The Aikido tenets of strength, power, relaxation, and relationships serve as the foundation for negotiation tactics that can be applied directly if a negotiation process becomes destructive.

Janet, a Quantum Leader, who worked in a male-dominated industry, was surprised by how well some Aikido practices worked in a difficult negotiation. She owned a small company, and her employees wanted to negotiate for more flex time. Although she intended to use a Quantum Negotiation strategy, she quickly found herself taking a strong position against the suggestions about flex time. Her first reaction was to think her employees required more, not less, discipline about their time.

Janet wanted to maintain a visible level of strength in her company and did not want to appear soft. She felt that her employees would take advantage of her if she agreed with them. She remained firm, and as a result, her employees became more oppositional.

As she prepared for a showdown, she remembered some of the Aikido and self-defense principles that she had learned in Quantum Negotiation. While it was difficult for her, she could shift her attitude and see the negotiation as less of a contest and more of an opportunity. She began to appreciate the differences between her and her employees' ideas about flex time. She remembered that resolving a conflict begins with an acknowledgment and continues with an appreciation of differences.

As in Aikido, she released the belief that she needed to be right or to control her group. As a result, she felt less burdened by the negotiation. She faced the conflict as a natural part of life, not as a contest between winners and losers. When she regained some emotional balance, and felt more positive about her employees, she thought with more clarity.

Her flexibility allowed her to move toward a willingness to lead a Quantum Negotiation with her employees. Janet and the team could come up with a plan for working on projects away from the office. Not only did the team become more productive, but Janet's satisfaction and enthusiasm also spread to her employees and led to improved morale in the office.

Stress in negotiation may pull negotiators more toward reactive, unconscious, and coercive choices. Like physical fitness, Quantum Negotiation's spiritual, social, and emotional fitness can build resilience and lead to faster recovery from mental and physical fatigue in a negotiation. Alignment, clarity, and awareness of our spiritual beliefs, social skills, and feelings lead to health and fitness for ourselves and enhances it for others.

Quantum Negotiation and Style-Shifting

There are many ancient and classic principles about the acquisition of power through shape-shifting to accomplish one's goals or to destroy an enemy. "Shed Your Skin Like the Golden Cicada" from the *Thirty-Six Stratagems of Ancient China*, for example, illustrates how to escape and regroup if you are in danger of defeat. There are sinister overtones—the strategy of most classic shape-shifting tactics is to use deception to destroy others. A coercive negotiator uses shape-shifting tactics to win at all costs in a negotiation.

These metaphors and myths about shape-shifting exist in many cultures. They traditionally demonstrate how someone can change their physical form to become another person or even an animal. The ability to transform and change shapes is an enduring, compelling human idea. When mythical characters, modern robots, or other creatures change their form or transform into a new shape, they create power, and thus obtain their needs and goals.

There are less fantastical, more practical ways that Quantum Negotiators can increase their power by using adaptability and style-shifting as shape-shifting techniques.

One of the most fundamental shape-shifting techniques that negotiators use is called style-shifting, which is defined as the ability of a negotiator to use a flexible set of behaviors and social engagement skills. The ability to style-shift helps to build rapport with a counterpart. For example, Negotiator A, who prefers discreet communication, plans to develop trust and rapport with Negotiator B, who is a very direct communicator. Negotiator A will learn to shift the discreet communication style to more direct communication. Rather than asking numerous questions, Negotiator A will prepare to deliver direct statements and ideas to match the style of Negotiator B.

Quantum Negotiators benefit from the paradoxical combinations of silence and strong communication skills; humility and self-confidence; quick thinking and reflection; caution and courage; and receptivity and resistance. A shape-shifter is buoyant and knows when to speak and when to be silent. Shape-shifting allows negotiators to share personal stories in a way that connects with others. Buoyant Quantum Negotiators can negotiate as events unfold, to be resilient, and to stand up for what they need.

A Quantum Negotiator shape-shifter can redirect strained or stalled engagement behaviors in a group. They can shift their style and attention in order to more fully engage everyone in their inactions. They can mindfully create "resonance" in the group by shifting the energy. It is much like a musician who can produce a sound or make instrument strings or voices vibrate in tune. This kind of energy is an invisible force that enables the group to get things done more easily. It is not like heat or thermal energy, or even the light from the sun; it is a kinetic and emotional motivation for movement toward common goals. Stamina and resilience are most often required for leading the energy or collective motivation of the group. However, energy referred to here is the "force field" of motivation and connection among partners or team members.

Quantum Leaders Manage Energy

Julia, a Quantum Negotiation practitioner, knew that she needed to shift her style and navigate her own and others' energy when her colleagues applied pressure tactics. She initially found it very difficult to change her preferred style of accommodation or "give in" energy. She did not like to use an assertive energy to state her needs. She did not like to persuade, trade, or use pressure with her employees or board members.

Today, however, Julia has found that with practice and reflection on her own behaviors, values, and emotions, she can transcend the comfort and habit of accommodation. She is now able to exercise a range of energy and redirect it at various times in a negotiation.

Julia today articulates her needs more directly, and is energized by her ability to accomplish more of her negotiation goals by shifting energy at different phases of a negotiation. In the past, she believed that using a more assertive energy seemed like "selling out" her own values to avoid conflict.

However, Julia was curious and desperate to be more satisfied in her negotiations.

Through the practices of Quantum Negotiation, Julia saw an opportunity for leadership development rather than a threat to her personal integrity. Julia transformed her "give in" energy to become more effective in her communication. She now prepares and practices "push" energy by being more direct about what she needs in negotiation. However, she knows that there is a time and a place, or a phase of the negotiation, when "push" energy is most effective.

Julia prepares for and can redirect and match the energy required at each stage of the negotiation process. She learned to use "pull" energy—asking questions, listening, disclosing information, and finding common ground in the preliminary phase. This creates an optimistic and positive climate where she and her colleagues find common interests.

Once the relationship is established, Julia is more confident to use "push" energy for the opening and closing phases of the negotiation where she can use persuasion, state her expectations, exchange ideas, and even exert pressure to establish her boundaries. She is now able to state without justification what she could give or not give in the negotiation.

Julia found that by using "pull" energy to clarify issues and establish mutual engagement, curiosity, and confidence in the relationship, she could use "push" energy to state her goals. This ability to manage the energy in negotiation creates a vibrant and creative exploration phase of joint brainstorming and problem solving. She learned how to leverage both the push and pull energy in the exploration phase, which creates a sense of inclusion and engagement for sharing great ideas and joint solutions.

With practice, Julia allows herself to be more attuned to her own intuition, a natural, organic capacity to perceive others even before they act or behave in a certain way. Julia "shifts" into the energy most supportive for engaging others during the negotiation. As a daily practice, she is able to sense when the dynamics change and how to redirect the energy to be more productive and engaging.

Julia's practice of her own pull-push energies develops and deepens her capacity to stay present while she engages in negotiation with others. Her anchoring or grounding allows her to adapt to disturbance and turbulence created by the situation or from her counterparts.

Julia is also able to "disengage" safely when she becomes overwhelmed. She learned to "move away" or walk away, postpone a discussion, take a break, meditate, or avoid an aggressive counterpart when the energy becomes imbalanced. She is comfortable adapting her style and redirecting her energy to accomplish negotiation goals not only for herself, but also for those with whom she negotiates.

The Quantum Negotiation community of practice is buoyant and knows when to use "push," "pull," or "move away" energy at different phases of a negotiation. Quantum Negotiators can negotiate when surprises surface, and can be resilient under pressure, thus achieving what they need with stamina and grace. For more detail on the definitions of "push", "pull" and "move away", see pages 80 to 81 in Part II Quantum Negotiation Tools.

Quantum Leaders Forgive

When there is an injustice or mistreatment in a negotiation, Quantum Leaders do not deploy revenge tactics to seek justice. Quantum Negotiators see acts of revenge as defensive acts in response to an offender's unwarranted and unfair behavior. If an offender makes a move that is unjust, even a Quantum leader will often feel the need to retaliate. In personal or professional negotiations, retaliation may take the form of refusals to cooperate, ignoring requests, or the use of exceedingly aggressive or legal tactics. Unlike a coercive negotiator, a Quantum Negotiator does not use revenge and retaliation in support of a winner-take-all mindset.

Thomas Asks:

Are you suggesting that if someone takes advantage of me and my organization, I should forgive and consider working with them again?

Quantum Leaders explore the skills and tactics of forgiveness to balance the power in an unfair negotiation situation. Forgiveness and revenge are two common human responses to unjust behavior. When someone believes that they have been the victim of an unjust attack, the coping responses are either to seek revenge or to forgive and let go of the negative emotions attached to the circumstances. Revenge can be passive-aggressive—refusing to provide needed resources, sabotage, or starting rumors. Or revenge can be direct—yelling, failing to protect another, or assault. In personal and professional negotiations, revenge actions often entail antisocial behaviors that will negatively alter the perpetrator's interpersonal effectiveness and reputation.·

Quantum Negotiators see forgiveness as a powerful alternative to most commonly held beliefs about injustice. However, the skills and discipline of forgiveness can conquer a situation that could potentially destroy your negotiation ability. Forgiveness is not about letting the perpetrator get away with something, but about increasing understanding of misconceptions and human shortcomings. The focus is not automatically on reconciliation with the offender, though it can be, but on repairing misperceptions within ourselves. Forgiveness is about choosing how to deal with manipulative behavior.

If you have been treated unfairly, it is normal to feel resentful or angry. Forgiveness skills, however, involve rethinking the meaning of forgiveness and your responses to intolerable negotiation circumstances. Forgiveness is a process that engages humans in a search for significance that is not clear in the situation. Some victims are not able to release their preconceptions about injustice. They become predisposed toward harshness and lack of caring. However, as insight is gained about a perpetrator's behavior and one's own psychological defenses, victims can reclaim their equilibrium and their vitality.

Rajan was a Quantum Leader in an architectural firm that was deteriorating due to his relationship with his business partner, James. He had been excited at first about the opportunity to create a partnership with another architect. Rajan did not know James very well personally, but he was familiar with his design work. Although both Rajan and James were invested financially and emotionally in their new company, Rajan soon experienced James's disrespectful and manipulative behavior. James rarely shared critical information with Rajan, and he used anger, fear, and guilt to intimidate Rajan.

When the partners needed to negotiate profit-sharing arrangements for the business, Rajan became particularly offended. James employed a range of aggressive tactics in a relentless push for further concessions to reduce Rajan's share in the profits. Rajan was attempting to lead a Quantum Negotiation, but in the face of such insulting behavior he too became aggressive and intransigent. He stopped listening to James. He no longer asked questions about James's interests. Rajan began to coerce James into making concessions and started to think about revenge and ways to get even.

Because of Rajan's intense need to be treated fairly, he had begun to use coercive tactics and to plot revenge. He planned a strategy of indirect attack. He would undermine James's legitimacy in the architectural community, sabotage his projects, and withhold needed resources and assistance.

Health problems and memory lapses began to dominate Rajan's life. His physician prescribed several mind-body techniques to combat his physical exhaustion. Rajan began to accept the fact that he was extremely resentful about the way James was treating him. He spoke with a colleague, describing the sense of injustice that he was feeling.

By talking with others, Rajan learned that James also wanted to find a way to resolve their differences, but did not know how. This stopped Rajan in his tracks. He began to consider the price that he was paying in health, time, and peace of mind by taking revenge. He decided to build a positive relationship with his business partner. Although Rajan did not know James well in the beginning, he took an interest in James's background and experiences. Rajan realized that it often takes years to forgive, but with mindfulness, he practiced a new way of thinking about his negotiation situation. He learned to observe the unity and interdependence of all tangible and intangible forces in the situation.

As Rajan prepared to listen more and state his own expectations more clearly, he became aware that he was ceding his power and reacting defensively. Rajan saw that his tactics of revenge and sabotage toward James were making him irritable and less effective in his professional interactions.

Rajan attended to the health of his mind, body, and spirit. He felt stronger in all three areas. Soon he accepted his share of the responsibility for exacting revenge in sabotaging James. Rajan forgave James for his aggressive behavior and forgave himself for acting like a powerless victim. He did not pardon or excuse James's manipulative behavior, but he could see that the relationship with James was in need of repair if their business was to succeed.

Rajan became less defensive and more energized. He realized that he had the spiritual and emotional reserves to apologize to James for withholding resources and assistance. The most significant realization occurred for Rajan when James relayed his own story about the firm's founding and how important it was to James that he be recognized for his original ideas and commitment to the success of the firm before Rajan had become involved. As he began to understand his partner more deeply, Rajan found it easy to recognize James's stature in the firm, and they moved to a profit-sharing agreement that was fair and equitable. Their reconciliation and Quantum Negotiation freed them to tap into their energy and uniqueness, which they used to make a success of the business.

★ ★ ★

Let's return now to the story of Ben, Amy, and John and the fight over the family cabin.

Fearing for the breakup of his family Ben marshaled his Quantum Negotiation skills and called John and Amy separately. Both spent most of the time telling Ben what they wanted and how they each needed to be assertive. Ben was patient and began to ask them about how they were feeling about the cabin or about the way they were treating each other, and why they needed to be right. What he helped them each realize was that the cabin represented recognition from the family that they mattered and how they would want their own children to experience the fun they had there.

Eventually, Ben got John and Amy together on the phone and they talked about the feelings and concerns they had for the family relationship. They all agreed that they needed to stay connected and be kind to one another, and respect everyone's desires. They each acknowledged John's ability to step in financially so their family could keep the cabin. Amy was grateful that John apologized to Ben for pushing him to sell his share so quickly. Since Ben was single and lived in Costa Rica, he did not need to make time at the cabin, but wanted to be sure he could stay connected with Amy and John even though both their parents were gone. He could visit them anywhere—it did not need to be at the cabin.

Next, John, Amy, and their children finally met to work out a more flexible scheduling and financial responsibility for the cabin. By bringing their adult children into the conversation, they could increase the communication for flexible scheduling and financial responsibility. In the end, they realized they could share some of the holidays and weekends at the cabin rather than exclude each other. Losing their parents was difficult and fighting over the estate had made them coercive rather than mindful Quantum Negotiators. By addressing their feelings and their human need to be recognized and connected, they could create an energizing family experience from the conflict.

★ ★ ★

Summary of HOW to Get What You Want and Need

To get more of what you want and need, you need to prepare for the HOW. Asking yourself the following questions will help with your preparation:

- How do you get what you want out of a negotiation?
- What are the strategies and tactics that you can use to achieve your goals?
- Are you going to use a classic or understanding approach?
- How do you integrate insights about yourself and your counterpart to develop a strategy?
- How do you assess the disparate needs and goals of each party?
- How do you use a Quantum Negotiation strategy to share critical quality information?
- How do you anchor your clarity to be buoyant in behavior?
- How does your strategy meet fundamental principles of durability, utility, and satisfaction?
- How do you measure your tangible and intangible assets?
- How do you respond to aggressive tactics?
- How do you identify narcissistic tactics?
- How do you adopt Aikido, shape-shifting, or forgiveness tactics?

By defining these Quantum Negotiation strategies and tactics, you are prepared for the negotiation and are more likely to get what you want.

By reflecting on the WHO, WHY, WHAT, WHAT IF, and HOW, you are now prepared for Quantum Negotiation experience. You know who you are, who your counterpart is, why you both are negotiating, what your goals are, what could happen if a negotiation breaks down, and how to get what you need by engaging with others. For more detail on the Quantum Negotiation preparation see page 79 in the Quantum Negotiation Tools.

We hope to have defined and illustrated in chapters 1, 2, and 3 how the mindsets and skillsets of Quantum Negotiation add value to negotiators and leaders alike. Your commitment to become a Quantum Leader will enable you to challenge and transform often stubborn beliefs, assumptions, and paradigms. As Quantum Negotiation is less about tactics and techniques, and more about how we show up, the relationship we create, and the energy we direct, it is those underlying beliefs and assumptions to which we turn our attention in the following section.

PART II

Quantum Negotiation Tools

For more information on training and coaching on Quantum Negotiation Tools visit www.quantumnegotiation.com.

Learn how Quantum Negotiation can have an impact for you and your team. There is an arsenal of solutions customized to your needs.

Negotiation and Leadership Development.

Schedule a Key Note speech.

Take the Quantum Negotiation Profile.

Schedule a Train the Trainer Certification.

Participants will walk away with a tool set of negotiation and leadership skills.

★ ★ ★

Understand and apply the essentials of cognitive, social and emotional elements in negotiation strategies.

Apply a deeper level of self and other awareness to improve interaction and negotiation strategies.

Use "power with" approaches for a more complete understanding of the interests and goals of all stakeholders.

Learn to style-shift while maintaining your own identity and values.

Use field analysis to optimize real life negotiation situations.

Figure Tools A.1 Power of Understanding—Preparation Framework.

VARIABLES	YOU	COUNTERPART	GAPS & COMMON INTERESTS
WHO a. Cognitive b. Emotional c. Social d. Physical e. Spiritual			
WHY a. Interests b. Needs			
WHAT a. Issues b. Objectives c. Limits & Targets			
WHAT IF Best alternatives if no agreement			
HOW a. Strategy b. Tactics			

Figure Tools A.2   Negotiation Behavior—Guidelines and Checklist.

PRELIMINARY STAGE   NOTES
- [ ] Take steps to establish a positive relationship
- [ ] Express optimism about outcome
- [ ] Point out areas of agreement and common interest
- [ ] Suggest agenda items and/or ground rules
- [ ] Clarify issues to be discussed and norms of negotiation
- [ ] Use situational questions to establish curiosity, mutual involvement, and confidence

OPENING STAGE
- [ ] State position or proposal clearly and concisely
- [ ] Support proposal with conviction
- [ ] Listen carefully to understand other party's proposal
- [ ] Ask questions to test other party's proposal
- [ ] Summarize areas of agreement and conflict
- [ ] Ensure problems on both sides are recognized & acknowledged
- [ ] Make certain analysis questions are positive and pertinent

EXPLORING STAGE
- [ ] Listen uncritically to encourage open discussion
- [ ] Ask many questions about the other party's needs and priorities
- [ ] Share "hidden" information about needs and priorities
- [ ] Ask about alternative currencies to meet needs
- [ ] Suggest alternative currencies to meet needs
- [ ] Ask implication questions to ensure the implementation of the solution is understood

CLOSING STAGE
- [ ] Make reasonable (rather than one-sided) offers
- [ ] Suggest alternative currencies to close gap
- [ ] Summarize the agreement to ensure understanding
- [ ] Keep exploring if others express concerns
- [ ] Clarify next steps before meeting ends
- [ ] Ask pay-off questions to establish customer benefits

© 2015 Quantum Negotiating

Figure Tools A.3   Pull–Push–Move Away Energy in Negotiation

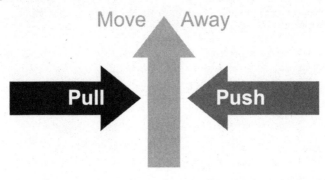

Figure Tools A.4   Push Negotiation Energy Examples

Figure Tools A.5   Pull Negotiation Energy Examples

Figure Tools A.6   Move Away Negotiation Energy Examples

Handling Hardball Tactics

This guide will cover how to deal with the most common hardball tactics:

- Belly-Up
- Boulwareism
- The Bully
- Dog and Pony Shows
- Forced Agreement
- Good Guy/Bad Guy
- Limited Authority
- Mad Max
- Passive-Aggressive Behavior
- Personal Attacks
- Phony Facts
- Silence and Patience
- Threats and Promises
- Uproar

DON'T BE A VICTIM—be anchored and buoyant!

Belly-Up

- These negotiators "acknowledge" the superior competence of those with whom they interact and say that they will place themselves in the hands of their fair and proficient opponent.
- Negotiators who encounter a belly-up bargainer tend to alter their initial position. Instead of opening with the tough "principled" offer they

had planned to use, they modify it in favor of their pathetic adversary, who praises them for their reasonableness, but suggests that his client deserves additional assistance.

- Belly-up bargainers are the most difficult to deal with, as they effectively refuse to participate in the process. They ask their opponent to permit them to forego traditional auction bargaining due to their professed inability to negotiate. They want their reasonable adversary to do all the work.

Action

- You must force them to participate and never alter a planned strategy in an effort to form a solution acceptable to such pathetic souls.
- When belly-up negotiators characterize initial offers as unacceptable, opponents should make them respond with definitive counteroffers.
- True belly-up negotiators often find it very painful to state and defend positions they espouse.

Boulwareism

- Boulwareism is associated with best offer first or take it or leave it bargaining. Insurance company adjusters occasionally try to establish reputations as people who will make one firm, fair offer for each case. If the plaintiff does not accept that proposal, the company will go to trial. Also called TAKE IT OR LEAVE IT tactic.
- Negotiators should be hesitant to adopt Boulwareism. The offering party effectively tells the other party that he knows what is best for both sides. Few parties are willing to accord such respect to the view of the opposing side.
- Boulwareism deprives the opponent of the opportunity to participate meaningfully in the negotiation process.

Action

- Negotiators presented with take it or leave it offers should not automatically reject them simply because of the paternalistic way in which they have been extended.
- You must evaluate the amount being proposed. If it is reasonable, accept it.

The Bully

- Such conduct is usually intended to have an impact similar to that associated with anger. It is supposed to convince an opponent of the seriousness of one's position. It can also be used to maintain control over the agenda.
- Those who try to counter an aggressive bargainer with a quid pro quo response are likely to fail, due to their inability to be convincing in that role.
- Negotiators who encounter a particularly abrasive adversary can diminish the impact of his techniques through the use of short, carefully controlled interactions. Telephone discussions might be used to limit each exchange. Face–to-face meetings could be held to less than an hour. These short interactions may prevent the opponent from achieving aggressive momentum.

Action

- A few aggressive negotiators try to undermine their opponent's presentation through use of interruptions. Such behavior should not be tolerated. When negotiators are deliberately interrupted, they should either keep talking if they think this will discourage their opponent, or they might say that they do not expect their opponent to speak while they are talking.

Dog and Pony Shows

- Some negotiators try to enhance their bargaining posture through printed brochures or video presentations. Brochures are often accorded greater respect than verbal recitations, due to the aura of legitimacy generally granted to printed documents.
- Those presented with dog and pony shows should not accord them more respect than they deserve. Negotiators should treat written representations just as they would identical verbal assertions.

Action

- If negotiators are provided with brochures before the first negotiating session, they should review them and prepare effective counterarguments, which they can state during discussions.

- Negotiators should not allow their adversary to use printed materials to seize control of the agenda. Where appropriate, they may wish to prepare their own dog and pony show to graphically depict their view of the situation.

Forced Agreement

- This technique can occasionally be used against win/lose opponents who do not evaluate their results by how well they have done, but by an assessment of how poorly their adversary has done.
- They are only satisfied if they think the other side has been forced to accept a terrible burden.

Action

- Although adroit negotiators may induce a careless, vindictive opponent to provide them with what is really desired, they must recognize that such a device will generally not work against a principled adversary.
- A typical win/win bargainer would probably accept the other party's disingenuous representations and provide them with the unintended result they have professed to prefer over the alternative that has been renounced.

Good Guy/Bad Guy

- In the Good Guy/Bad Guy routine, a seemingly reasonable negotiator professes sympathy toward the "generous" concessions made by the other party, while his partner rejects each new offer as insufficient, castigating opponents for their parsimonious concessions.
- Single negotiators may even use this tactic. They can claim that their absent boss suffers from delusions of grandeur, which must be satisfied if any agreement is to be consummated.

Action

- Negotiators who encounter these tactics should not directly challenge the scheme.

- Those who interact with Good Guy/Bad Guy negotiators tend to make the mistake of directing their arguments and offers to the unreasonable participant to obtain approval, when it is often better to seek the acquiescence of the reasonable adversary before trying to satisfy the irrational one.
- It is always important when dealing with unreasonable opponents to consider what might occur if no mutual accord is achieved. If the overall cost of surrendering to such an adversary's one-sided demands would clearly be greater that the cost associated with not settling, the interaction should not be continued.

Limited Authority

- Many people like to indicate during the preliminary stages that they do not have final authority from their company about the matter in dispute. They use this technique to reserve the right to check with their company before any tentative agreement can bind their side.
- Bargainers who meet opponents initially claiming they lack the authority to bind their company may find it advantageous to say they also lack final authority. This will permit them to "check" with their own absent people before making any final commitment.

Action

- Negotiators who suspect that an adversary might use this technique may wish to select the one or two items they would most like to have modified in their favor. When their opponent requests changes, they can indicate how relieved they are about this, because their own company is dissatisfied. Then they can offer to exchange their items for those their adversary seeks. It is fascinating to see how quickly the opponent will now insist on honoring the initial accord.
- The limited-authority situation must be distinguished from the one where an opponent begins a negotiation with no authority. This adversary hopes to get several concessions prior to actual negotiations with an authorized decision maker.
- Negotiators should avoid dealing with a no-authority person, as he is trying to induce them to bargain with themselves.

Mad Max

- If negotiators become angry, they are likely to offend their opponent and may disclose information that they did not wish to divulge. Negotiators who encounter an adversary who has really lost his temper should look for inadvertent disclosures which that person's anger precipitates.
- Negotiators often use feigned anger to convince an opponent of the seriousness of their position. This tactic should be used carefully, as it can offend adversaries and induce them to end the interaction.
- Some negotiators may respond with their own retaliatory diatribe to convince their adversary that they cannot be intimidated by such tactics. A quid pro quo approach involves obvious risks, as a hostile exchange may have a deleterious impact on the bargaining.

Action

- Negotiators may try to counter an angry outburst with the impression that they have been personally offended. They should say that they cannot understand how their reasonable approach has precipitated such an intemperate challenge. If they are successful, they may be able to make the attacking party feel guilty and embarrassed, shaming the person into a concession.

Passive-Aggressive Behavior

- Instead of directly challenging opponents' proposals, passive-aggressive negotiators use oblique but highly aggressive forms of passive resistance.
- They show up late for a scheduled session and forget to bring important documents. When they agree to write up the negotiated terms, they fail to do so.

Action

- Those who deal with a passive-aggressive opponent must recognize the hostility represented by the behavior and try to seize control.
- They should get extra copies of important documents just in case their opponent forgets to bring them. They should always prepare a

draft of any agreement themselves. Once passive-aggressive negotiators are presented with a fait accompli, they usually execute the proffered agreement.

Personal Attacks

- The other side may use verbal or nonverbal communication to make you feel uncomfortable. They can comment on your clothes or your appearance.
- They can attack your status by making you wait for them or by interrupting the negotiations to deal with other people. They can imply that you are ignorant.
- They can refuse to listen to you and make you repeat yourself. They can deliberately refuse to make eye contact with you.

Action

- Recognizing these tactics for what they are will help nullify their effect on you, and mentioning them explicitly will probably prevent a recurrence.

Phony Facts

- The oldest form of negotiating trickery is to make a knowingly false statement or misrepresentation of the facts.
- A practice of verifying factual assertions reduces the incentive for deception, as well as your risk of being cheated.
- Don't call the other party a liar, and don't allow him to treat your doubts as a personal attack. Rather, make the negotiations proceed independent of blind trust in the facts.

Action

- Deliberate deception is quite different from not fully disclosing one's thinking. Good faith negotiation does not require total disclosure.
- The use of a neutral third party as a confidential sounding board can often determine whether there is a zone for potential agreement without having to fully disclose sensitive information.

Silence and Patience

- Many negotiators fear silence, because they are afraid that they will lose control of the transaction if they stop talking. The more they talk, the more information they disclose and the more concessions they make. When their opponents remain silent, such negotiators often become even more talkative.
- When negotiators have something important to say, they should say it and then keep quiet. A short comment accentuates the importance of what they are saying and provides the other party with the chance to absorb what was said.
- This rule is crucial when an offer or concession is being made. Once information has been disclosed, it is time for the other side to respond.

Action

- Patience can be used effectively with silence. When the other negotiator does not readily reply to critical representations, he should be given sufficient time to respond. If it is his turn to speak, the first party should wait silently for him to comment. If the first party feels awkward, he should look at his notes. This behavior shows the silent party that a response will be required before further discussion.

Threats and Promises

- Threats are intended to show recalcitrant parties that the cost of disagreeing with offers will transcend the cost of acquiescence.
- Pressure often accomplishes just the opposite of what it is intended to do; it builds up pressure the other way. Instead of making a decision easier for the other side, it often makes it more difficult. The question changes from "Should we make this decision?" to "Shall we cave in?"

Action

- Good negotiators rarely resort to threats, as there are other more effective ways to communicate the same information. If threats are to be effective, however, they must be believable.

- Instead of using negative threats that indicate what consequences will result if the opposing party does not alter its position, negotiators should consider affirmative promises that indicate their willingness to change their positions simultaneously with the other party. The classic affirmative promise, the "split the difference" approach, has been used by most negotiators to conclude a transaction. One side promises to move halfway if only the other side will do the same.

Uproar

- A few negotiators try to obtain an advantage by threatening dire consequences if their opponent does not give them what they want.
- For example, a board in negotiations with an employees' union might say that it will have to lay off one-third of the employees due to financial constraints. It will then suggest that it could probably retain everyone if the union would accept a salary freeze.

Action

- Negotiators confronted with such predictions should ask themselves two crucial questions:
  1. What is the likelihood that the consequences will occur?
  2. What would happen to the other party if the consequences actually occurred?
- In many cases, it will be obvious that the threatened results will never happen. In others, it will be clear that the consequences would be as bad or worse for the other side as for the threatened party.
- Bargainers occasionally may have to call an opponent's bluff. If union negotiators were to indicate that they could accept the layoffs if the board would only raise salaries for the remaining employees by 30 percent, the board representatives would probably panic. They know the company could not realistically function with such layoffs. They were merely hoping that the union would not come to the same realization.

PART III

Quantum Negotiation Mindset

4 | Independence Is a Powerful Illusion

Katie was proud of her promotion to senior project engineer—and rightfully so. She was the first woman in this role in her company and the decision to choose her for this position was a testament not only to her competence but also her tenacity. She was excited about the project portfolio she was entrusted with; it included a number of high-visibility projects of strategic importance to the growth of the company. She had learned that success for a woman meant being overprepared and ready to prove herself at any time, and she was determined to succeed, even if she had to double-down on her preparedness. She knew that she would be watched very closely and had to prove to a good number of skeptical men that she was up to the job.

But Katie was determined to exceed expectations, even as she was transitioning into her new job. She woke up even earlier than she usually did to make sure she was on top of all the developments, and she was the last to leave the office, tying up loose ends and steeping herself in the various details that could represent risks to project completion. She sacrificed not only her sleep, but also family obligations and friendships. Her promotion also meant that some of the teammates with whom she had been close before her promotion were now her direct reports. She started to maintain a certain professional distance, which she thought would help her manage them better.

After a few weeks, Katie felt she had achieved a good grip on the various projects she had been entrusted with. She felt comfortable making decisions and directing her team, and raised the performance standards across her projects significantly. She also introduced a number of changes that would allow her to monitor the project implementation more closely, so that she could intervene when she felt it necessary, particularly when it came to resource allocation and utilization, as well as supplier selection.

However, when she was just about three months into her role, she noticed that the error rate had shot up, timelines were slipping, and she had to override many more decisions than in her previous two months. When three of her best reports gave their two weeks, notice in the same week, she became alarmed. With the loss of these key people, the completion dates for two of the projects were in serious trouble. She was getting increasingly panicked, and, as was her habit, she put even more work on her shoulders.

When Paul, one of her previously close teammates, stepped into her office unannounced to tell her that he was considering leaving the team to take a similar role with a different business unit, she lost control. "What is going on here?!" she yelled. "I am working like a dog picking up all the loose ends to make us all look good in the end . . . and then people are abandoning the ship! Even you, Paul? I don't understand!"

Paul took this opening to give Katie some much-needed feedback. "You know," he started, "you are not the same person that we knew from before your promotion. You don't trust us anymore. You override many of our decisions, or make them yourself without even consulting us. Then you get upset if we are not fully on board or simply executing what you had decided. You are micromanaging us! We are losing confidence in ourselves, and frankly, we are starting not to care about our work anymore. You were always driven, but now you have become maniacal. If you do not make a change fast, we're all going to leave, and good luck with that."

Paul hesitated, worried that he had crossed a line. But someone had to tell her. He realized that Katie had sat down and was seriously thinking about what he had said.

He continued, "You need to trust our judgment and experience again; don't double-check all of our work, or override our decisions without even a discussion or conversation. We are wasting a lot of time on reports to you that we wouldn't need if you simply trusted us and our judgment, and let us update and consult with you where it counts."

He hesitated again; then added: "Remember, we are all in this together, this is not just your show!" With that he left her office, feeling that she probably needed some time to think by herself.

To develop the mindset and skillset of Quantum Leaders (and negotiators), we need to contend with some deep-seated beliefs and assumptions that implicitly inhabit our worldviews. When we confront them consciously, equipped with insights and examples, we can unlock surprising sources of success.

One such notion is the belief that the successful leader or negotiator—akin to an individual hero figure—is a self-sufficient maverick who resourcefully outsmarts others in the pursuit of maximum gain and glory. This is Katie's affliction and that of many others who are also reinforced by organizational culture and processes—including performance management systems and expectations that are overly individualized. Embedded in our heads and systems are powerful assumptions about independence and interdependence. And we can all benefit from the voice of a Paul to make us stop and reflect. Once confronted, and we have contemplated and adjusted, the foundation for quantum capabilities becomes well anchored.

New and Improved Framework

Reliance on independence is founded on a win-lose perspective about power. If my sole goal is to be independent or to use Machiavellian approaches, I may lose out on satisfying relationships or community support for my interests. I do not need to exercise power over others in a competitive way because we all are more secure if we uncover our practical common goals.

There are intangible and often invisible sources of power, such as courage, discipline, and resilience, to engage others to help me. By focusing on being too independent, I miss out on the ways others can help me accomplish my goals. Failing to do so can also mean I have less satisfying relationships and little meaning, purpose, and value in my social and professional life.

The ideas of interdependence and interconnectedness are anything but platitudes. They deserve serious consideration. In fact, much has been said here already about the interconnected world we live in today. There is mounting evidence in physics, neuroscience, genetics, and cultural anthropology about the nature of interdependence on all levels of our human existence. The field of negotiation is another field where the Newtonian world of "power over" matter and people is no longer a reality. Newtonian science believed that atoms are separate and can be controlled in a linear, command-control, predictable way. In negotiation, it was proclaimed that we would be rewarded with efficient, fear-based, reward-punishment strategies.

However, quantum science has uncovered the interconnected web of subparticles below Newtonian matter, which is multidimensional, unifying, unseen energy. As in negotiation, actors are not separate and isolated from one another; they are, in fact, part of one interdependent whole of a relationship, team, or organization. This concept has provided astonishing insights about how to get more of what you need in life. The skill is in making the choice to be conscious of the social, neurological, and strategic interconnectedness in daily life, and manifesting that consciousness in how we engage with those we seek to influence.

Today's leaders and negotiators cope in an ocean of uncertainty, turbulence, disruption, and cultural shifts. Rather than focusing on the goal to survive as an independent winner in a such a world, Quantum Leaders are aware of structural, systemic trends and can embrace the uncertainty and anxiety in their human nervous system by remembering how unified they are at the quantum level. They have more success, satisfaction, and energy in meeting their needs, getting support, and enjoying life's resources. As a result, they create sustainable and resilient outcomes.

Neuroscientists have discovered that the social brain is uniquely sensitive to our unseen world. Globalization is reshaping our brains, helping us to become more aware of the realities of interdependence. Globalization has affected the patterns of cognition, curiosity, and adaptive ability for successful global negotiators. Quantum Negotiators think it is important to manage and shape global conditions in response to increasing interdependency. For example, adaptive skills include thinking about the shared national interests in terms of the physical environment and resources, and the ways protectionism can harm international trade.

Scientists studying systems and deep ecology point out that from a system point of view, the only viable and sustainable solutions are those that meet mutual and immediate human needs. A system point of view asserts that there is a broader understanding that one country's national interest or security is linked to the physical, economic, and social forces of other countries. In a similar fashion, negotiators who develop social intelligence can facilitate agreements that satisfy the immediate needs of a negotiation problem without diminishing the prospects for future prosperity.

With mindful consciousness, Quantum Negotiators understand and practice new behaviors in order to adapt and influence their social interactions in a constructive way. They increase their ability to cooperate by recognizing other negotiators as fellow problem solvers rather than as adversaries. This goes against the classic coercive power negotiation attitude of rivalry. Digging into a position or taking a defensive stance in a negotiation can undermine the willingness of others to cooperate. Before they make a proposal, it is important that they uncover their unconscious attitudes and beliefs about defending and separating themselves from others.

Independence versus Interdependence

Freedom, self-sufficiency, and independence have been glorified as the ultimate social, economic, and political goals throughout Western human history. Devotion to, reliance on, and responsibility for others have also been universal themes of philosophers, economists, and social scientists for all time. Maybe today we have just become more aware of the pluses and minuses of experiencing accelerating interdependence.

Just like the individual personal need to feel independent and free, countries pursue competitive, protective measures to avoid devaluation, deflation, or pollution in the context of interconnection. Interdependence, rather than rules, underlies the basis of all societies (unless there is complete isolation). There are many studies claiming that it is the interconnectedness among peoples that has led to sustainable evolution and success.

At the global realm, individual negotiators and institutions have developed ways for further economic interconnectedness through shared laws about communication, transportation, technology, and dynamic flows for goods, capital, people, and services.

For government, organizations, leaders, and individual contributors, negotiation skills are needed to coordinate more complex and integrated issues than ever before. Everything moves at a speed and in volumes that would have been inconceivable just a decade ago. The benefits of low interest rates, cheap commodities, and access to information at a global stage have an impact on daily life for most of us more than ever.

There is disruption in the foundations of industries, economies, and the power balance between buyers and sellers, and new competitors are rapidly shifting. Global interdependence and antiglobalization are creating more uncomfortable and even destructive changes and unseen possibilities for negotiators.

It is no wonder that our human nervous system is often anxious and uncertain. Quantum Leaders have learned that mastery of interdependence is a key skill to living in our modern world. The ability to get what you need—including tangible and intangible goals, and collective and personal ones—is essential. Global interdependence has increased the opportunities and challenges in working with others from around the world.

Wendy Asks:

So how, then, can I become more interdependent?

Katya, based in Poland, has experienced the tension of interdependence in her multicultural virtual team working for a US global company. For several months, Katya and her five other team members were grateful to receive significant leadership training about how to communicate in a global team. Team members committed to practices of listening, self-reflection, and mindfulness. This was especially important because of the social and geographic distance in virtual teams. Such a global team requires a deep understanding of their mutual needs and how to collaborate for success.

Katya's team was intentional about the need to cooperate, to be accountable, and to support the collective— and sociocentric—team goals.

However, Katya soon shocked herself when she did not practice her Quantum Leadership skill to manage conflict and respect in the team.

At one difficult meeting, the project deadline was looming, the team call was past her bedtime, one of the team members (Maria) did not attend due to a medical emergency, and two team members (Li and Antonio) from the United States had just left a disturbing meeting at the corporate office about possible layoffs.

Li led the call with agenda setting and stating the goal of getting to firm action steps in this meeting. However, Antonio hijacked the meeting by taking the agenda off track toward his individual issues; commenting on how poor Li's English was; blaming the other team members for not delivering the quality Antonio was expecting; and repeating some gossip he heard about Maria's medical issue.

Li tried to facilitate the meeting as best he could. Katya, however, was hoping that Mei (the other team member) would speak up; when she didn't, Katya let Antonio's behavior pass, as it was getting late and everyone was stressed. She knew that stress can trigger a default tendency to thinking only about their own interests, which could lead to defending themselves against one another. She was surprised how quickly she and her team members did just that.

After the meeting, Katya was ready to blame everyone else but herself. In her initial reflection, she blamed Li who had been too accommodating. She blamed Antonio who had become even more aggressive as Li backed down. Katya wished she had spoken up and behaved more as a Quantum Leader to support Li and the team, but she hadn't. She soon realized that she had not practiced her mastery of interdependence and had neglected to remind the team of their mutual goals and vulnerabilities.

Katya then reflected on how she could lead a reengagement of the team to enhance rather than destroy their social network. Without it, the team would become even more stressed and would not meet their goals of tangible project completion or intangible satisfying relationships. By following the Quantum preparation model, she led the next call more effectively.

Katya facilitated a discussion to review their behavior without judgment or blame. She led the meeting by highlighting the shared interests they all had and reminding them that they could give, share, or ask for help about their own frustrations. The team became much more energized and respectful as they asked questions and expressed optimism about their relationships. By focusing on the relationships and mutual needs, Katya's team found areas of agreement and common interest and learned that physical stress can also affect the quality of their interactions.

Mastering Sociocentric Self-Interests

Katya's example highlights the nature of personal development required to master interdependence or to achieve collective goals. Mastery in the context of interdependence requires a deeper understanding of the unseen attitude and mindset about self-interests. When our self-interest is understood in a sociocentric way, using "ends justify the means" tactics will only destroy important trust and relationships in social networks.

Wendy Asks:

I am really good at my job and feel like I deserve the recognition that I get when I close a deal. Why should I not take credit for my own work?

Quantum Negotiators consciously manage their own behavior in preparation to influence and lead others through specific behaviors (how they act) and cognitive practices (how they think). With this intentional Quantum Leadership method, negotiators enhance their power because of their ability to self-correct and encourage constructive behaviors in social interactions. Quantum Leaders are conscious of their behaviors through self-observation, goal setting, and self-rewards. Clarity and anchoring about their self-interest as being mutual with a counterpart leads to more efficient, satisfying, and sustainable agreements and relationships.

When mastering interdependence, Quantum Negotiators break from traditional Machiavellian tactics to get "followers" to focus on and comply with a leader's goal. These "power over" tactics require external compliance (i.e., "carrots, sticks, persuasion") techniques. This traditional focus sacrifices the time and energy devoted to clear recognition about how negotiators' own self-interests affect others around them. Quantum Negotiators start with a practice of honest reflection about their own interests, and strive to see those interests in the context of the collective.

Even under the limitation of time, capital, and resources, Quantum Negotiators reengineer or reinvent negotiation practices to include a focus on mutual goals, rather than solely defending individual wins.

Quantum Leaders recognize that most negotiations require social engagement skills, which combine not only claiming value, but also creating value practices. Where there is limited time, resources, or capital, they expand the perception of finite resources because of their disciplined and creative negotiation skills. In quantum physics, all subparticles are available everywhere and always, and only need to be recognized and organized with intention.

The goal is not to become completely self-reliant, autonomous from others, or to win relative to others. This may not seem admirable and exciting to some, but it is not realistic or relevant for twenty-first-century negotiators. Quantum Negotiators acquire leverage more realistically through the laws, norms, and practices of cooperation versus competition. Seeing the world exactly as it is today means to recognize and leverage positive social relationships as a method of reaching success and improving one's own self-interests and prosperity.

Interdependence and Social Capital

Like Katya, Quantum Negotiators understand the reality of interdependence and the ways to create, value, and measure the impact of social capital. In addition to assessing the tangible outcomes in a negotiation, such as the value of the deal, or resources benefited, Quantum Negotiators value and assess their intangible social capital. The trustworthiness of their networks and relationships increases the collaboration, support, and sharing that others provide to them. An emphasis on building social capital recognizes the quality of information that results from positive and satisfying social networks and relationships. A Quantum Leader knows that to increase positive social capital, they make a choice to attend to every interaction as an investment in emotional, strategic, and spiritual rewards. Through their deliberate attention and care, their social capital grows in value over time.

In order to build positive social capital, Quantum Leaders share information, coordinate activities, and make shared collective decisions. They know that in a mutual-gains negotiation, a reputation of fear will not generate social cooperation. Attention to trust-enhancing behaviors will lead to social resonance, positive energy, and rapport within and across negotiation teams. This increases the potential for critical information sharing. Because interdependence is the reality, Quantum Leaders are aware of the ways that each person can help the others to understand and solve problems.

. In most negotiation situations, the informal disclosure of information is required before effective action can be undertaken. Sustained positive social relationships and networks are the most effective way to gain access to useful information that might otherwise be hidden because attention and time are limited resources. A quality investment of time in relationship management contributes to an internal coherence for negotiation partnerships or groups. When agreements and relationships enhance a sustainable future for a contract and relationships, the value of their reputation and life satisfaction increases significantly. Constructive social relationships improve negotiation outcomes and result in less costly dispute resolutions.

Non-Zero-Sum Interdependence

A zero-sum situation is when one's gains are balanced by the losses of a counterpart. If the total gains of the negotiators are added up, and the total losses are subtracted, and the sum equals zero, this is the classic "power over" negotiation. Some organizational or national cultures traditionally reward aggressive zero-sum maneuvers, which encourage heavy-handed game playing and manipulative tactics. These negotiators will never share information (or quality information). They will use every means possible to undermine the will of a counterpart. They will use whatever emotional, behavioral, and physical tactics they can to devalue a counterpart and make them yield. This "power over" approach glorifies the individual negotiator who can have a strategic and, sometimes intuitive, understanding of where a counterpart is vulnerable.

Quantum Negotiators reengineer these tactics of pushing counterparts' buttons, emotionally upsetting them, or using vulnerabilities against them.

These destructive and coercive tactics do not foster working relationships and do not produce the glue of trust that is required for economic and social institutions to work properly.

Quantum Leaders know that predatory and coercive tactics can become retaliatory and hostile. These tactics can result in stalemates or exacerbated tensions, and are against leaders' own emotional and spiritual needs. In addition, in the classic Evolution of Cooperation model, actors who claim value, defect rather than cooperate, and use "power over" others to achieve short-term gains with undesirable and unintended consequences. Quantum Negotiators have learned that there are more and better options available to them and that it is easier and more effective to focus on practices to build satisfying relationships in interdependence. They know that, rather than depleting limited resources, it is in the collective interest to create value through cooperation, coordination, and equitable division of resources.

Wendy Asks:

What kind of value do I actually gain from working with my counterpart?

Quantum Leaders have learned how important it is to develop new skills for creating value, as opposed to simply claiming value. They want to cooperate with their counterparts in negotiation. Their self-interest is protected and advanced when they choose clarity and intention to conquer fear and egoistic protection. Quantum Negotiators require not only knowledge but a mindful practice to think systematically about creating value in negotiation. Value can be created even in the most straightforward sales, such as finding aspects other than price to explore options that satisfy the parties.

Quantum Negotiators also explore intangible needs and values, such as delivery time, quality, and relationship, to create value and opportunities where none existed before. Practices, expectations, and strategies that create value cultivate innovative outcomes and satisfaction in social interactions. This in turn helps to overcome panic, misplaced superiority, and naive optimism. Quantum Leaders invest in understanding interdependent self-interests in complex negotiation situations, because doing so is the most practical and effective mechanism possible for allocating resources, balancing competing interests, and resolving complex conflicts.

US-Mexican Interdependence

Cross-national public and private Quantum Leaders are represented in many governmental organizations facing geographic and economic interdependence. The Arizona-Mexico Commission (AMC), for example, works in partnership with the Comisión Sonora-Arizona (CSA—its Mexican counterpart). Through Quantum Negotiation they collaborate through strong public and private advocacy to increase binational trade, networking, and information exchanges.

The Arizona-Mexico Commission has made a significant difference in the Arizona-Mexico region since its founding in 1959 by Governor Paul J. Fannin, who stated, "God made us neighbors, let us be good neighbors." These Quantum Negotiators are anchored in their own national values and buoyant in their behavior to accomplish great things despite the change in national political administrations over the years.

The AMC–CSA joint sessions illustrate the best of cross-cultural Quantum Negotiation practices to advance higher living standards, with improved public safety and better flow of goods and people at the border. The committee's leadership and advocacy start with the commitment by individual members to take time to reflect on the often-unconscious cultural dimensions that can disrupt ambitious plans.

Not only do these committee members negotiate important policies for the region, but they also act as a vehicle for conveying these messages to decision makers in Washington, DC, and Mexico City. The members focus their negotiation efforts with one another on advancing policy priorities, including competitiveness, sustainability, security, and quality of life.

These complex initiatives involve concerted efforts not only between various levels of government, but also across different sectors of society within the two countries. To have impact, the members took time at their sessions to reflect on how they think, behave, and feel as cross-cultural leaders. They took the time to understand that culture is founded on many identity levels—national, organizational, committee, and individual.

The focus on shared interests and cross-cultural awareness practiced by the committee members includes attention to what has been learned and expected by each of them from their own unique cultural perspectives. They learned to see their beliefs and behaviors as culturally bounded and socially conditioned. They actively engaged and supported each other in expanding their understanding and behavioral repertoire, including new negotiation practices. Particularly when culturally diverse relationships are involved, the ability to grow and integrate new perspectives and behaviors is key.

This requires both cognitive flexibility and behavioral agility. This agility requires us to "unlearn" many of the past habits that are no longer effective. When we encounter different ways of engaging with others who have different behaviors and preferences, we become aware of how ineffective our own preferences are in gaining trust. The ability to "unlearn" some of our past behaviors we have relied on take a flexible mindset. "Relearning" new behaviors and new ways of communicating in new social contexts takes a lot of behavioral dexterity.

Some key skills to enhance these Quantum Leaders' success include cultural due diligence, dialogue about differences, mentoring one another, and individual style-shifting. These negotiators represent the best of mastering interdependence in creating and implementing sustainable strategies to innovate by including diverse viewpoints. In an era of economic and political disruption and exponential change, Quantum Leaders negotiate with intention, reflection, and collaborative action.

Vigilance and Interdependence

Our interdependent, global landscape is often described as volatile and disruptive to the strategies and plans of leaders and organizations. Where a marketplace is changing rapidly and new competitors are emerging overnight, leaders need to widen their observation and negotiation skills. Quantum Leaders have learned that it is necessary to go beyond traditional scenario planning and measures of success. There is a need to constantly track continuous change outside their organizations, and to tap into diverse networks both within and outside the organization and across multiple boundaries. This vigilance requires negotiators to "see" disruptive forces before it's too late.

For Quantum Leaders, vigilance is a deeply disciplined practice of observing and listening to what might be, what differs, what confounds, and what challenges lie ahead. The ability to be buoyant is then possible when the reality of multiple and mutual interests is understood as our social reality. That is, we have shared interests with others who can assist us in getting what we all need.

With vigilance to the changing landscape of mutual interests, Quantum Leaders know how to use "power with" emerging new actors in the global or industry landscape to successfully achieve their goals. By consciously attending to interdependent social, economic, and spiritual interests that emerge, they can maintain quality relationships and innovate mutually beneficial outcomes.

Quantum Leaders are vigilant in constructive and inclusive behaviors to accomplish mutual goals. They engage in joint information sharing and problem solving, and recognize the shared feelings of others in a social context. Mastery in the context of interdependence is more than the ability to get along well with others and to enjoy the benefits of others' support and generosity; that is, it's more than "people or interpersonal skills." Quantum Leaders have a social intelligence that includes awareness of human dynamics that nourish relationships. They invest in developing relationship skills to increase their knowledge about interaction styles and strategies that help them achieve their objectives when negotiating with others.

In the context of interdependence, Quantum Leaders know that they can have an impact on others across a spectrum from "damaging" to "nourishing" effect. Therefore, there is a reengineering away from tactics of deceit and manipulation that make others feel devalued, angry, frustrated, guilty, or inadequate. Quantum Leaders are vigilant in using behaviors in relationships that make others feel valued, respected, affirmed, encouraged, and competent. This nourishing behavior tends to make Quantum Negotiators more powerful because they become, for example, more effective in communicating, connecting, or problem solving with others.

In fact, we have observed that for Quantum Negotiators, interdependence is not a state, but an action—a deliberate practice. Mastering it involves self-monitoring individual thoughts and feelings that may be offensive or harmful to others while attempting to nurture relationships. Besides self-monitoring, the practice of interdependence also involves fine-tuning the reality of a relationship and cultivating sociocentric self-interests in social situations; that is, cultivating a sense of "we." Quantum Leaders understand that they are not separate but part of a social whole.

Attention to the impact of one's own behavior, along with clarity and empathy about social conditioning that others may have experienced, can increase Quantum Negotiators' powerful ability to engage and influence others. Rather than take a primarily self-focused view when interacting with others, Quantum Negotiators understand others' perspectives with empathy and awareness of their own impact on others—this manifests in curbing impatience, eliminating distractions by phones or other devices, reducing defensiveness and/or blaming others for their own anxiety, for example.

Powerful creativity, empathy, compassion, and conflict-resolution skills require an understanding of mutual needs and the nature and quality of relationships. When interdependent self-interests are explored, and validated in friendships and teamwork, Quantum Leaders have the power to know that people become more engaged, exploratory, and energized in their behavior as a result. In this way, others are enthusiastic to support Quantum Leaders who are socially intelligent. The more someone can help others to achieve their goals, the more they help others feel valued and supported, rather than leaving them feeling defeated or devalued. They know that destructive relationships can be toxic and have a negative impact on their own brain chemistry, immune systems, resilience, and overall health.

Remembering Interdependence in Negotiation Preparation

Richard was engaged in a four-year negotiation to craft a real estate marketing agreement with a client. He managed the business development aspect for his firm, while his partner ran operations.

The client, "Top Sales," met often with Richard. Jim, the team leader, was a "listener and observer" in the meetings. Kenneth, the main negotiator, consistently took an outspoken, protective, and defensive approach. He continually expressed concerns about the risk they faced in the contract terms. As the architect of the new project and the contract terms, the third member, Sonny, was more focused on a quality working relationship. However, in meetings with everyone present, Sonny allowed Kenneth to take the lead. Because of the negotiation dynamic between the three of them, it took "centuries" for Richard to complete an agreement.

As Richard prepared for the negotiation to discuss updating contract terms, he was committed to the Quantum Negotiation approach. In the past, Richard could not negotiate well when Kenneth aggressively complained about setbacks in the execution of contracts. It was often difficult for Richard to think clearly about the mutual needs that he shared with Kenneth. Richard was determined to have a frank discussion to find ways to improve these unproductive meetings. He needed to clarify his needs and communicate them effectively under the uproar.

Richard's company had incurred significant talent recruitment and training costs based on the promise that "Top Sales" would have the necessary digital system in place to support the marketing work his company would do. Kenneth refused to acknowledge the fact that his own company had not lived up to its part of the agreement and shared responsibility for poor performance. Kenneth's tactic was to dominate the discussion by blaming Richard's company.

Richard drew on his Quantum preparation of WHO he was and how interdependent he was with "Top Sales." In the past, Richard would default to thinking how to become more independent, protective, and tricky in maneuvering around Kenneth. Richard recognized how the stress was making it difficult for the entire group to negotiate.

By focusing on their interdependent goals, Richard could be supportive and engaging with the group throughout various months of meetings. Soon he noticed how the interactions shifted from extremely tense to more open and exploratory. Richard did not try to change Kenneth, but he continued to explore "Top Sales" goals and how they could be improved with Richard's marketing resources and ideas.

Richard continued to think in a nonjudgmental and empathetic way. Instead of judging Kenneth's defensive tactics and seeking to change them, he chose to style-shift for better communication. He also observed that when his own need to protect himself surfaced, he started to doubt himself and felt powerless. He continued, however, to practice aligning himself on his five human dimensions. Kenneth was relentless in disregarding their mutual needs. Even on the day of signature, Kenneth stalled and made additional demands. Richard remembers how empowered he felt when he did not try to control Kenneth's behavior, but kept his focus on the interdependent goals.

Something "clicked" for Richard on the day of signature. He could finally appreciate the fact that he would not be sitting there ready to sign a lucrative contract if he wasn't the "right person" for "Top Sales." Richard paused, then said to the team, "Can you possibly think of a better person to do this for you than me?" Pause. "I know you can't think of someone." Suddenly, there was a thunderous laugh and Jim, the observant team leader, said, "I love Richard and the way he talks! It's a deal." They all shook hands, and continue to execute the contract to this day.

Richard's satisfaction increased significantly when he reflected on how he behaved, and he felt a sense of integrity between his own spiritual and strategic intentions and his actions. Richard experienced having a positive impact on the working relationship and clarity about not only his needs on the contract, but also how to support "Top Sales" in their growth. He feels connected to something vital and collective now as he works with "Top Sales."

Leaders like Richard can generate an "emotional contagion" that spreads because it meets an underlying social need to connect, be understood, and be supported. In the context of their shared interests, he helped to synchronize the group's tense emotions to shift toward a more collaborative dynamic. By synchronizing his expressions, vocalizations, postures, and movements with Kenneth, Richard could influence Kenneth's willingness to cooperate. Richard's nonverbal behaviors of listening, clarifying, and joint problem solving had an impact on Kenneth's innate willingness to agree to mutually satisfying goals.

This may seem like a counterintuitive suggestion, but if we demonstrate vulnerability, then we are humanizing the situation and inviting somebody else to show up as vulnerable, which leads to greater levels of trust and connectedness. This is powerful, particularly when vulnerability is paired with perspective, which means truly being inquisitive and trying to understand what the world looks like from another's perspective. Doing so breaks down barriers—especially when we do it with empathy, not just out of intellectual curiosity, but with the intent to create a relationship based on mutual understanding.

Summary

Independence is indeed a powerful illusion. It is upheld and reinforced, particularly in individualistic cultures and systems that downplay the social dimension and celebrate individual achievement and accomplishment as self-made. In such systems, performance, success, and failure are assigned, measured, and evaluate individually. Often the responsibility to and concern for the social contexts (or group), are treated as discretionary and unmeasured acts of benevolence. The search for independence is indeed a powerful bias or force of human nature to protect ourselves against others, especially in times of resource and time limitations. This often dominates the unconscious bias in many business environments, organizations, and management/leadership philosophies today.

However, the (re-)emergence of "the social," through social media, and the shifting emphasis on teamwork and collaboration of late, may not be a surprise, but certainly impose a tension into individualistic legacy systems that requires careful reconciliation. The emphasis on teamwork and collaborative behaviors—however strong—is still a far cry from proactively practicing interdependence, such as negotiation skills.

Challenging the notion and mindset of independence and deeply integrating the reality of interdependence into our belief system, perspective, and outlook is essential. And, independence or the state of complete individualism and protection of the self is only the first of three key biases to examine. The next one relates to our reliance on surface appearance and impressions when making sense of situations and planning our response. As we will see, tuning in to the hidden, unseen forces in negotiations, and staying attuned to them, holds surprising transformational power.

5

What You See Is Not What You Get

A delegation from a major Moroccan financial institution was excited to meet with EquiTech (ET), a UK-headquartered fintech company, to negotiate the terms of their business relationship. ET's advanced technology platform seemed best suited to meet their needs for enhanced security, speed, and reliability of certain financial transactions. They were chosen from among three contenders, including one from France and the other from Germany, whose technology promised similar advantages. What distinguished ET was their customer support—well, supposedly.

Already, after the first day, the Moroccan delegation was ready to pull out. Their executives were incensed at the rude and disrespectful reception by their host. Their conduct and lack of courtesy and attention to their guests did not match the promises of being focused on customer needs. That evening a junior member of the delegation communicated to the ET team how displeased the Moroccan executives were and that they were considering withdrawing from the negotiation.

This news puzzled and surprised the ET team. The conversations had been friendly and pleasant, although a bit less substantive than the team expected. They were prepared, and they presented at great length the specifics of the arrangement, the anticipated updating and upgrading cycles, project implementation plans, and even offered to train their prospective client's staff at no additional cost in order to address gaps in their technical competence. Overall, it was a good day.

The only curious occurrence was the extreme task and business focus of the delegation. Simon, the ET team had expected to start the meeting with a more informal lunch to "break the ice," establish rapport, and get more personally acquainted before turning to the business at hand. With an empathic comment and question ("You must surely be hungry after this early morning flight. Would you like some lunch?"), he bid the delegation to lunch. However, Simon and his team were very much taken aback when the head of the delegation refused, stating that they were not hungry at all.

Simon tried again about forty-five minutes later, after his initial presentation to set the stage for the technical reviews to follow, but his offer of lunch was refused again. Simon, together with his increasingly hungry team, was wondering if this refusal was part of a negotiation tactic to negotiate further concessions later on that day. He was perplexed that this prospective client was threatening to withdraw. After all, the technical reviews went very smoothly and his team could answer all the questions and challenges the delegation had raised.

He was worried now. What did they miss? A lot was riding on landing this deal. They were not as big as their competitors, and they invested heavily in developing this opportunity. Landing this deal with this semigovernmental client would bolster their credibility and open up opportunity in fast-growing markets in the region. A lot was at stake and they had been focused and prepared. Simon was getting anxious and wondering what went wrong.

Robin, a subject matter expert on the ET team mentioned that this threat might very well be a hardball negotiation tactic. She had heard that North African negotiators were shrewd, calculated, and unpredictable. She mused that even though they had seemed very pleased with the technical aspects of the meeting, they might just be setting the stage for a hard-nosed fee negotiation the next day.

Simon appreciated the comments but found little consolation in them. After all, they had negotiated the fees before and had been very transparent about the cost structure and the impact on margins. Surely, their prospective client could appreciate how slim the margins would be, particularly through the initial startup phases. Then, they also threw in the training at no extra charge, which was a considerable investment of ET time and resources. What else could they want?

The evening conversation on the Moroccan side was very different. The leaders of the delegation, a member of the Royal family among them, were incensed by the disrespect they had experienced. They traveled to make this deal and did not even get the courtesy of lunch! One of them said that he expected nothing less than this disrespectful treatment, as this was to be expected by such cold and insensitive people. "It's typical! Just look at their history!" he exclaimed. Emotions were clearly high.

$$\star\ \star\ \star$$

Quantum physics is the science of the invisible (and surprising) aspects and forces that make up reality. Similarly, Quantum Negotiation (and Quantum Leadership) entails being alert and attentive to the seemingly small and invisible aspects that underpin human thinking, feeling, and behavior.

Throughout most of the twentieth century, social and biological studies on the invisible workings of the human brain and human behavior were seen as incompatible. Scientific advances now focus on a synthesized approach across diverse sciences. Quantum physics and social neuroscience both emphasize the connection between the different levels of social and biological domains (for example, molecular, cellular, system-related, personal, relational, collective, societal, and cultural). Social neuroscience investigates the connection between neural and social processes developed in social psychology, cognitive psychology, and neuropsychology. These approaches are associated with a variety of neurobiological techniques, including functional magnetic resonance imaging (fMRI), transcranial magnetic stimulation, electrocardiograms, endocrinology, and immunology.

What researchers are learning about the human brain and how it functions has direct application to how Quantum Negotiators learn, and retain what they learn, as well as how implicit associations and unconscious biases affect the process and outcomes of negotiations. In addition, the socially conditioned brain (i.e., the social mind) has been decoded. Neuroscience research has also shown that social learning can be more robust than individual learning. Quantum Negotiators gain clarity on how they learn from their own social conditioning and how this may contrast with the way others have been rewarded as they learned. This knowledge serves as the foundation for effectiveness and helps manage conflicts both at work and in their personal life.

So, how does that help us understand the derailment experienced between the Moroccan delegation and the ET team?

Had both parties been more attentive to the "quanta" in their interaction—the seemingly small and invisible aspects that underpin human thinking, feeling, and behavior—this experience might have unfolded very differently. Both parties failed to factor in the nuances in their respective cultures and prevailing norms that determined expectations and behavior. They lacked awareness of their own and the others' socially conditioned brain. This included the biases and stereotypes that are deeply embedded in our cognitive frames, yet easily evoked and reinforced through stress.

What the ET team failed to comprehend was refusing an offer for lunch was a respectful and polite response from a Moroccan perspective. The expectation was that the host would continue to offer and then cajole the host into accepting the lunch invitation and move to the lunch area. Declining the offer was simply the first step in a polite ritual that would allow the guest to maintain a sense of propriety and modesty while allowing the host to emphatically manifest the best of their intention—their care, concern, and esteem for their guest.

The importance of this "dance" and its implicit meaning in a culture where honor, giving face, and saving face—which means showing respect and avoiding shame and embarrassment—are key drivers for behavior and motivation cannot be underestimated. That lunch was ready and waiting did not make a difference; the insult and lack of sensitivity of the host who left their guest hungry by not being attuned to the interactive intricacies, however, did.

The clash with the expectations and assumptions for the ET team could not be greater. The intricacy and meaning of this dance was simply absent from their more pragmatic frame of reference about lunch and explicit understanding of the answer to the statement "You must be hungry!" In addition, the pushy way of cajoling violated senses of propriety and respect from their cultural perspective.

Most critically though, neither side recognized the nature of these gaps, but fell victim to stereotypes and biases that are deeply anchored in their respective collective unconscious. The attitudinal shifts thus created can have a profound repercussion, change the course of relationships and negotiations profoundly, and undermine even the best of intentions. In this case, a French competitor ended up with the contract. It was the historical connection between the two countries that anchored greater levels of attunement to such relational "quanta." The lack of insight and astuteness, and sensitivity derailed a mutual-gains strategy.

The following experience shared by Juliette and Marcus illustrates how they could find mutual gains both at work and at home by reorienting from a self-focused view to the smallest particles of their shared interests.

Juliette and Marcus had a personal relationship, as well as a partnership in a small business. As Quantum Negotiators, they wanted to use a mutual-gains process to negotiate at home as well. Their relationship was tested under the stress of competing work demands. Their schedules were in conflict, they both put in long days, and the financial stress of a new business was putting a lot of pressure on them. The rapport and trust that had kept them going in the beginning were deteriorating.

The needs and demands of the business left Marcus and Juliette with little time or energy for themselves or each other. Their feelings of frustration and lack of motivation began to affect their business, their marriage, and their health. The frustration was creating confusion and uncertainty about how to solve challenges in the business. It was also blocking the emotional and physical energy they once brought to the partnership. Increasingly, they were losing clarity about each of their own needs, which had an increasing impact on the business partnership. The more the business relationship became strained, the less personal energy and vitality they had, and vice versa.

As Juliette and Marcus reflected on their emotional, spiritual, and physical dimensions, they began to understand their feelings and behaviors more fully. They became more aware of not only their own emotional needs, but also joint needs of their relationship and business. They discovered that it was necessary not only to advance the interests of the business, but also to have separate identities and boundaries about their individual needs—to be sociocentric, separate but connected. They created a psychological safety for them to share and exchange their deepest needs.

As an introvert, Juliette was easily overwhelmed by the social networking demands of the business. When she understood and accepted her need to recharge her batteries with quiet time and contemplation, Juliette became much more energized and creative, proposing new ideas and plans for the business.

Juliette negotiated for needed quiet time to boost her energy. This time balanced her need for quiet, belief in service, behavior as a partner, and her ability to think more creatively about the business.

Marcus recognized that his need as an extrovert was to spend more time with other people. He negotiated to take over the sales and marketing element of the business. Energized by the social activity of meeting with potential buyers, Marcus knew that he needed activity to recharge his enthusiasm for the business. Both sets of talents that Juliette and Marcus provided were required for the success of their business. Their goal was not to think alike, but to think together. This has become an important tool of their negotiation success. They restructured their business to include and engage the best of their talents and needs.

Smallest Particles of Motivation

Marcus and Juliette's experience illustrates key aspects of human motivation. Research points out that modern humans are motivated less by the classic carrot-and-stick approach than by having their emotional needs about choice and self-actualization engaged. This understanding of how to motivate others is one of the primary Quantum Leadership skills and creates psychological safety for sharing information.

An obstacle for many negotiators who think they need to use coercion is that they are often unaware of how complex their needs really are in a social interaction. As a result, despite all their preparation, they often do not really understand what motivates them to behave the way they do and why a relationship is important to them. Therefore, they have not clarified all the unseen motivations that they have of their own. When clarifying on both the personal and the social needs they have, they can enhance their careers and relationships.

The unseen needs of the relationship helped Marcus and Juliette to negotiate more successfully. Juliette, for example, took the time to think about and to ask Marcus what his emotional, spiritual, and physical needs were. She did not just think she knew what he wanted. Because she had experience and insight from doing this for herself, she had the capability to recognize, validate, and respond to what Marcus needed. This clarity in their understanding of the multiple levels of needs they each had increased their effectiveness in negotiating and supporting each other.

Wendy Asks:

How can Quantum Negotiators help their people to be motivated to experience a change like this one?

Quantum Negotiators know that humans are largely driven by intrinsic personal rewards and motivations, and not by controlling or coercive forces in partnership dynamics. The classic coercive tradition of making threats does not motivate friends or colleagues very well to comply with requests or demands in relationships. Those who use Quantum Negotiation behaviors are becoming increasingly aware of how and why internal rewards encourage cooperation.

A sociocentric orientation of self-interest provides the insight necessary to guide powerful leadership in a dialogue versus a debate by engaging, listening, and keeping in mind the interests of both parties. Quantum Leaders do not abandon their own goals for the sake of others, as an altruist would. A sociocentric orientation helps those most powerful to realistically acknowledge that their own and their partner's self-interests are connected. This encourages nourishing behavior in social interactions, as accepting and listening to a friend can motivate him or her to be more trusting and cooperative in solving problems. Blaming, reprimanding, and invaliding a friend's concerns does not.

Anxious or controlling individuals are unlikely to recognize that the self-interests of colleagues are in fact compatible. Tragically, then, with too much control they often reject a rich resource of relationships that would help to support life's goals. Quantum Negotiators recognize themselves as autonomous, but still interconnected, in making decisions and fulfilling their life goals.

Thomas Asks:

You have given me some good tools to work with, but I get really anxious when I need to negotiate something important. What can you suggest I do to overcome that?

Quantum Leaders explore the unseen ways that disruption in their external environment affects or causes disruption in their own internal nervous system. By understanding the unseen ways their human brain works under stress, these negotiators gain clarity about the way they think, feel, and behave. Research in brain science can be applied in negotiation preparation by being more conscious about what threatens or makes them anxious.

By embracing the natural human response to fear, they can consciously create a safe climate for shared experiences and ways others can cocreate solutions. The Quantum Preparation framework is a great tool to calm their own anxiety with knowledge about the seen and unseen dimensions of negotiation. This creates less motivation to control others out of fear, but rather to respond in ways to create safe and collaborative relationships.

One of the Quantum Negotiation practices is to explore unseen adaptive, defensive ways that negotiators often fall into under high stress. When it is understood that a fearful reaction can create a disconnection from themselves or others around them, negotiators prepare to be anchored and connected to their own needs and manage their own anxiety first. Without consciously aligning and anchoring their own emotions, body sensations, memories, and senses, it is natural that negotiators would depersonalize others and go on autopilot to control and coerce others without a recognition of any lost value creation.

Quantum Leaders connect and anchor to their surroundings and have clarity about others' perceptions of reality. This anchoring of their own identity and needs prevents confusion, uncertainty, or conflicts when expressing what they need. This anchor is the foundation for their buoyant behavior in stressful, turbulent relationships or circumstances. The conscious practice to explore how their own mind is the source of anxiety, and how it affects their own and others' brain chemistries and connections, instills confidence and patience in others. Preparation in understanding why they might have a racing heartbeat, panic attacks, lightheadedness, and other physical symptoms in the presence of a counterpart can then be managed with more clarity.

Karine's Preparation for Leadership Anxiety

Karine shared a story about how she used the Quantum Preparation framework to manage her own anxiety before taking a leadership position in her career. As a Quantum Negotiator, she knew she needed to manage her own anxiety before she could effectively lead others. Before she went to college she had planned to be engaged with others in the dorms and classes. She knew that the single rooms with long corridors would require her to break her habit of "keeping herself closeted up." She had a lot of perceptions about her "social anxiety" and preferred to be alone, avoid social conflicts, and to "mind her own business."

Karine believed that her shyness kept her from engaging with others. She preferred to go to the movies by herself and spend her study and free time alone. However, she wanted to have more fun and learn to be more social and engaging in her freshman year. She had a good friend who encouraged her to take her time, to "trust herself," and to get comfortable with who she was. He also said she should notice that all the new freshmen had common interests and concerns. This gave her a sense of her connection to her own needs and how to begin engaging with others.

Once she learned to appreciate and connect with her own identity, she became clearer about her goals and the ways her anxiety kept her from connecting with others. First, she learned to accept that she did not like loud parties, music, and alcohol. Then she began to make friends in small groups and she soon found herself more included in the freshman community.

However, she noticed that she could not get what she needed in some groups that were controlling and disrespectful. She would want to say something about the disrespectful way people talked to one another, but she did not feel confident in herself. Karine knew that she would like more leadership positions on campus but was anxious about speaking up. Karine found it was hard to feel satisfied or reach her goals of achieving better social connections and visibility in her first freshman semester because she would avoid all conflict situations.

Her avoidance in speaking up for her needs and for others created more stress for Karine and she was soon excluded from many campus groups. She then sought out an internship at a mental health facility on campus. In her classes and training, she learned mental health practices and tools she could use to help others. By learning new communication skills and ways to advocate for others, she could negotiate for many of her patients with the administration and community centers. By managing her own anxiety and developing her negotiation skills, she felt empowered to make a difference where she had felt avoidant or indifferent before. Today, Karine uses her Quantum leadership and negotiation skills as a clinical mental health counselor, yoga instructor, and expressive dance therapist. Here are just a few of the steps she used to increase her leadership capability:

1. Take a more observant look at social relationships and WHO you are in relation to others in that context
2. Observe and gain more clarity about WHO others are in your social circles and WHY their behaviors don't necessarily mean they are suspicious or malevolent
3. Take responsibility for the choices and feelings of WHY you do not often engage with others
4. Explore WHY others have similar interests and needs and WHY relationships can be engaging and supportive
5. Consider WHAT IF there is a situation you choose not to engage in, what alternatives and options you do have to disengage
6. Prepare for HOW you could connect to others, understand differing perspectives, and lead engagement with them

The Unseen: The Culturally Conditioned Brain

Quantum Negotiation practices are built on what social neuroscience teaches about the human nervous system and what underlies human health and behavior. Humans are fundamentally a social and connected species, rather than isolated "atoms," to parallel what quantum physics has discovered. Cultural groups evolved with the neural and hormonal connections to support them, and this helped communities, families, and societies survive and grow. The way the human brain develops is dependent on and susceptible to cultural influences and stimulation. Culture becomes the unseen pattern of ideas and emotions that are shared among members of a group and renders their behavior and symbology meaningful and coherent.

Quantum Negotiators explore what they unconsciously learned and how they expect and reward the same cultural behaviors. Deliberate focus on emotional regulation and clarity in thinking assists Quantum Negotiators to optimize their brain function and fitness for the possibility of releasing trust chemicals and building a functional whole-brain circuitry to perform, problem solve, share limited resources, and to create new things, even under stressful conditions.

Quantum Negotiators are also aware of how to connect with, inspire, and influence others to collaborate and cooperate, by understanding how contagion of either positive or negative dynamics can "infect" a group and influence it's developing (micro-)culture. The clarity of one's own cultural values, integrity, and presence will have either a positive or negative impact on others' ability to maintain the same. If a Quantum Negotiator has a positive impact and builds strong relationships with his team or counterpart, then they will be able to renegotiate time and time again as their industries, organizations, and markets rapidly change.

The Quantum Negotiation Profile (QNP)

A conclusive body of research points to the detrimental impact of unconscious bias in cultural groups, and organizational and leadership performance. The QNP identifies a negotiator's cultural orientations and flags similarities or gaps with others that can either contribute to undesirable disconnects or desired synergies in relationships. It helps make conscious the unknown attachments, beliefs, and assumptions that have an impact on our success. With this awareness, Quantum Leaders can better navigate these unseen forces through adaptive behaviors and strategies. This practice of cultural competence is at the heart of buoyancy.

This tool can assist negotiators in understanding the hidden, cultural, conditioned drivers of subjective experience—motivation, beliefs, assumptions, interpretations, and behaviors. It serves as a discovery tool to build the awareness of self and others upon which the successful calibration of

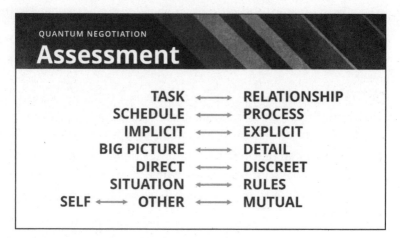

Figure 5.1   Quantum Negotiation Profile.
©2015 Quantum Negotiation

one's relationship, leadership, and negotiation behaviors depend. It is based on seven scales of cultural dichotomies that factor, mostly unconsciously and implicitly, into the conditioned calculations and assumptions. Figure 5.1 provides a brief summary for easy reference. Engaging with these scales helps make the unconscious conscious and explicit so that we can use this awareness deliberately to enhance the quality and success of our interactions. To receive training or coaching along with your own Quantum Negotiation Assessment go to www.quantumnegotiation.com.

1. Task–Relationship Centeredness

This scale relates to fundamentally different approaches to problem solving and taking action. See Figure 5.2 for a graphic representation.

A task-centered approach is characterized by a focus on the essential issue to address or problem to solve, and attempts to pursue the most direct path of action to accomplishing a specific outcome. This approach prioritizes the most efficient way of getting things done. In contrast, a relationship-centered approach focuses on the relationships that surround the issue or problem and are involved in achieving a specific outcome. This approach prioritizes the building of trusting relationships as a foundation to

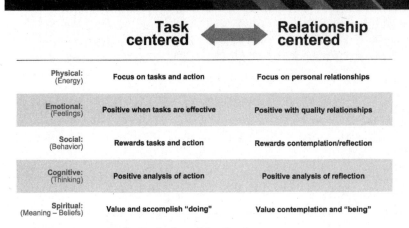

Figure 5.2   Task–Relationship Scale
©2015 Quantum Negotiation

getting things done. From a relationship-centered perspective, relationships cannot be separated from the task at hand. From a task-centered perspective, relationships are secondary and subordinated to the task at hand, often more discretionary than mandatory.

These differences have a powerful impact on negotiation behaviors, even on the very definition of negotiation itself. Do we understand a negotiation as a transaction, or a deal, that is primarily achieved at the bargaining table? Or is it a relationship and therefore requires the careful orchestration of a relationship? Interculturally, the understanding of and approaches to negotiation reflect this difference. In relationship-oriented cultures, bargaining—which is often deemed to be the essence of nego-tiation in task-oriented cultures—is but a part of the overall negotiation process that is nestled within carefully orchestrated relationship strategies that can seem entirely nonessential to the task-oriented negotiator.

For example, when Jose from southern Mexico began working in the United States in New York, he felt uncomfortable with getting right to the task at the beginning of meetings. He was more comfortable from his background to spend a lot of time at the beginning of meetings to discuss family and weekend events. There was more of a focus on the task rather than on the relationship and he learned to regard this as not better or worse, but different from what he was used to.

2. Schedule–Process Focus

This scale is related to how negotiators relate to and use time. It distinguishes two fundamentally different foci that define how we orient ourselves toward time. See Figure 5.3 for a graphic representation.

A schedule-focused approach values detailed planning, schedules, and timelines, and values their adherence. They value punctuality and feel that time commitments are fixed, unchangeable, and that agreed-upon schedules determine actions. In this approach, time is an independent variable. A process-focused approach is comfortable with an unfolding and ambiguous process that requires responsiveness and adjustment. In this approach, time is a dependent variable. Schedules, timelines, and time-bound commitments may shift and adjust in light of new requirements and information impacting the evolving process.

Negotiations are inherently dynamic and uncertain, but the need to exert control over them through schedules can create a sense of certainty and urgency into the process. As such, schedule orientations are more cor-related with task-oriented negotiation approaches, whereas a process focus is commensurate with a relationship–based understanding of and approach to negotiation.

	Schedule focused	**Process focused**
Physical: (Energy)	Time determines action	Actions determine time
Emotional: (Feelings)	Positive precise definition	Positive loose definition
Social: (Behavior)	Rewards precise definition	Rewards loose definition
Cognitive: (Thinking)	Positive analysis of precise	Positive analysis of loose
Spiritual: (Meaning – Beliefs)	Value binding timelines	Value a flexible/relative process

Figure 5.3   Schedule–Process Scale
©2015 Quantum Negotiation

3. Implicit–Explicit Communication

This scale refers two different orientations toward communication, specifically how we encode, decode, and exchange meaning. Figure 5.4 provides a graphic depiction.

An implicit approach to communication is likely to value metaphoric, artful communication, including indirect references, understatements, humor, as well as nonverbal (intonation, facial expressions, etc.) and extraverbal (settings, use of space, gift giving, and other symbolism) ways of conveying meaning. Implicit communicators expect and scan for hidden meanings within communication. This tendency can easily clash with explicit communicators who generally rely on words for meaning, verbal or in writing, and discount the importance or significance of nonverbal and extraverbal aspects of communication.

In any communication, including negotiations, implicit and explicit aspects coexist. As contexts evolve, conventions and norms dictate the reliance on more or less explicit approaches. Formal negotiations are often expected to result in a contract, which gives expression to mutual expectations, obligations, and entitlements of each party explicitly in writing, and ratified through signatures. The process of arriving at a

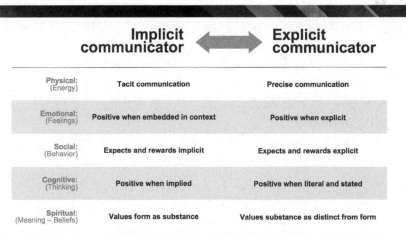

Figure 5.4 Implicit–Explicit Scale
©2015 Quantum Negotiation

written contract, however, often starts in more implicit ways. Of course, an agreement more often takes the form of a confirmatory e-mail, an emoji, a handshake, an "OK" gesture, a thumbs-up, a head nod, shared clapping, participation in a prescribed ritual or rite of passage, a meal together, a simple toast, or conforming with set rules and norms. These signals of implicit agreements and understanding among parties are the results of a negotiation process that was never perceived or labeled as such. The degree to which we resort to explicit forms of agreement is often a function of existing trust, perceived risk, and complexity of an agreement, such as the number of stakeholders, or the size, scope, and significance of the agreement.

4. Big Picture–Detail Orientation

This scale refers to different cognitive approaches and uses of logic and argumentation. Figure 5.5 provides a graphic representation of these key cognitive styles.

A big picture–oriented approach focuses first on the larger context of a situation/task. With this approach, there is an individual focus on agreement on general frameworks and principles that will then, by inference and extension, also apply to the specifics of a given problem or situation. They are

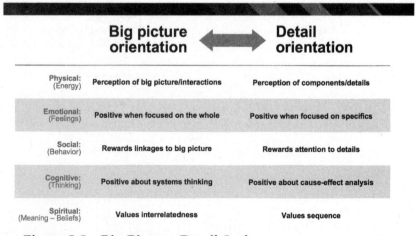

Figure 5.5   Big Picture–Detail Scale
©2015 Quantum Negotiation

likely to think broadly and generally, looking at the interdependency and patterns between variables, and focus on their complex relationships. This contrasts with a detail-oriented approach, which focuses on the specifics of a given situation or problem, isolating the specific variables of significance. Negotiators leave the surrounding context and interrelated variables out of scope and narrow in on the precise aspects under investigation or negotiation.

We can discern vastly differing approaches to negotiations between those oriented toward the big picture and those oriented toward details. The types of questions asked early in a process provide cues about the preferred approach of one's counterparts, for example. Does she raise questions regarding the context or features of a specific solution to be agreed upon? Does she notice features or frames? Does she notice the setting in which interactions take place or is she focused just on the discussion?

5. Direct–Discreet Conflict Handling

The scale relates to different styles for handling conflict. Figure 5.6 provides a graphic representation of the key differences.

A direct conflict-handling style is likely to be open and straightforward in conflict situations. Direct conflict handlers speak their mind openly and

Figure 5.6   Direct–Discreet Scale
©2015 Quantum Negotiation

may not be worried about the impact on others, assuming that honesty about thoughts and feelings is of primary value to a relationship. Direct approaches can vary significantly in their "emotional loading," that is, the degree to which emotional expression is considered an important aspect of the valued honesty. By contrast, discreet conflict-handling approaches are likely to prioritize face-saving and the appearance of harmony, honor, and respect throughout conflict situations. This is accomplished by suppressing open discord and resorting to more indirect modes of communication in conflict situations, such as the use of intermediaries, as well as the use of allegories or understatements and implicit communication (see earlier discussion). Discreet conflict handlers tend to withhold and guard their true thoughts and feelings in conflict situations.

Negotiations and communications always entail a form of disagreement, friction, or conflict and the act of resolving them to the satisfaction of all stakeholders. Hence, conflict-handling approaches are integral to negotiations. Sensitivity to and compatibility of conflict approaches among stakeholders are significant factors in success.

6. Situation- and Rule-Based Approaches

This scale refers to differences in criteria that guide decision making. Figure 5.7 graphically depicts these different approaches.

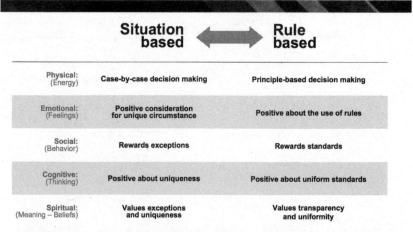

	Situation based ⟷	**Rule based**
Physical: (Energy)	Case-by-case decision making	Principle-based decision making
Emotional: (Feelings)	Positive consideration for unique circumstance	Positive about the use of rules
Social: (Behavior)	Rewards exceptions	Rewards standards
Cognitive: (Thinking)	Positive about uniqueness	Positive about uniform standards
Spiritual: (Meaning – Beliefs)	Values exceptions and uniqueness	Values transparency and uniformity

Figure 5.7   Situation–Rule Scale
©2015 Quantum Negotiation

Situation-based approaches tend to be highly pragmatic and variable, depending on the specific situations encountered and their constituent variables. By contrast, rule-based approaches tend to set or adhere to specific rules that govern decision making regardless of specific situations. When confronted with a rule, a situation-based approach is likely to reinterpret the rule, feel it needs to be adjusted to the situation, or ignore it altogether, if it seems too broad and general.

For a process-based approach, it is likely that negotiators want to adapt their behavior based on the situation. They may feel that rules should be adjusted to better suit a situation. A rule-based approach is likely to regard rules as binding independent of a situation, and it abides by rules, processes, and regulations as the guidelines of behaviors and choices. For rule-based individuals, rules provide consistency and the understanding of expectations.

This difference affects negotiations in a significant way as the very principle of negotiability may be perceived differently through the differing lenses of situation- and rule-based approaches. From a rule-based perspective, rules are nonnegotiable. They are the very foundation for reliability and trust, and govern formal and informal, explicit and implicit agreements. From a situation-based perspective, however, rules themselves are subject to interpretation and negotiation as a situation-based approach can precluded the acceptance of a seemingly general and abstract set of rules in circumstances that may make the rules appear meaningless or irrelevant.

This also extends to the understanding and "binding" nature of a written contract. It is common for many businesspeople to experience surprise, when upon the completion of contract negotiation in countries with a more situation-based approach, the counterpart continues the negotiation even after a formal contract with clear terms, conditions, and rules has been signed. This behavior makes perfect sense from a situation-based lens, particularly if circumstances and conditions around the agreements have shifted.

7. Self-, Other-, or Mutuality Focus

This dimension does not parallel the other scales as it depicts three fundamentally different interests that drive decision making and understanding of

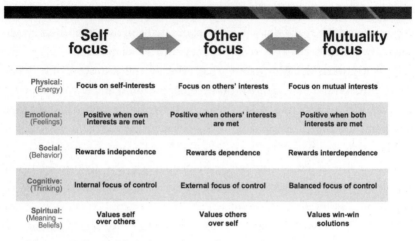

Figure 5.8   Self–Other–Mutuality Scale
©2015 Quantum Negotiation

gain and motivation. Figure 5.8 provides a graphic depiction of these three approaches.

A self-focused approach prioritizes the pursuit of individual interests and needs. It assumes that maximization of gain and furthering of self-interest are the most common, natural or desirable motivations in the interactions and exchanges between people. Self-focused approaches tend to value independence and self-reliance, and approach negotiation with a sense of more or less adversarial competitiveness. It is often in this competitive assumption where the respect is earned through particularly skillful, sometimes cunning, tactics. By contrast, an other-focus approach focuses on furthering the interest of a counterpart's interests as a way of harnessing value. The success of this approach relies on the assumption of reciprocity. By furthering another's goals and well-being, the other is or becomes equally motivated. This approach tends to value dependence and obligatory exchange among interacting agents.

A mutuality-focused approach is focused, from the onset, on mutual benefits and opportunities. This approach is based on the recognition of interdependence among the parties in an exchange. It recognizes the self-interests of each while also recognizing and respecting the needs and interests of the other. They value interdependent relationships that further all stakeholders' interests and well-being, for as long as mutual value and win-win outcomes can be sustained.

The relevance of this scale to negotiation and leadership is obvious. Negotiations, whether formal or informal, tend to work best when the parties involved share an assumption about how interest is pursued. The competitive nature of self-focused approaches, when shared between stakeholders, can be quite complementary and yield mutually satisfactory outcomes. But when matched with the other approaches, the result may be distrust and disrespect, and lead to misunderstanding and disappointment as a result.

These scales indicate some measure of difference for understanding and approaching negotiations. They characterize individual preferences in the workplace, as well as organizational and socially enshrined beliefs and norms that can either enable or derail success. Quantum Negotiators and Leaders not only understand these differences and their international and intercultural contexts on individual, group, and organization levels, but they also apply their understanding in practical terms. A Quantum Negotiator's competence relies on the practice of meta-skills, which we have identified and defined as:

Cultural Due Diligence: This is the habit of assessing cultural similarities and differences and anticipating their potential (desirable and undesirable) impact. This can be done by inviting into the planning process people familiar with the cultures involved and who can provide comparative insights. Studies and tools can also provide useful comparisons, as well as specifically commissioned cultural diagnostics or cross-cultural, due-diligence assessments. The latter is particularly recommended when large ventures and transactions are at play, such as joint ventures, mergers, or acquisitions. The Quantum Negotiation Profile also provides a useful framework to organize comparative assessments.

Frame shifting (also: perspective taking): This is the ability to understand the perspective, worldview, and experiences of others from their vantage point and with their frame of reference. While cultural due diligence is typically a rather more clinical and objectified undertaking, frame shifting adds the important subjective, psychological, and emotional dimension to our understanding of differences. This skill requires empathy and emotional intelligence.

Without frame shifting, cultural due diligence is insufficient, as it does not make accessible the all-important human dimension in our trans- and interaction. Through our intercultural work, we are convinced that the high failure rate of organizational transformations and cultural integrations (as in post-merger & acquisition) are due to either the absence of cultural due diligence or the reliance of a purely clinical, objectified comparison. Seriously factoring the subjective experiences and perspectives of all parties involved into our planning and relationship strategies enables surprising results, even breakthroughs.

Style-shifting (or style agility): This is the ability to translate insights and understanding of cultural differences into adaptive behaviors. Doing so requires a broad and flexible cognitive and behavioral repertoire. Style-shifting is immanently learnable, but requires self-awareness and deliberate practice of behaviors and approaches (and associated beliefs) that expand our culturally conditioned comfort zone. Style-shifting is not only an individual skill, but also a capability of teams and groups in order to navigate differences and/or adapt to shifting requirements and circumstances.

We have developed the Quantum Negotiation Profile as a self-assessment tool to ground the development of style-shifting. The results alert the Quantum Negotiator to the invisible and unseen forces that have an impact on success. The results indicate an individual's "range," that is, the part of the scale that defines the individual's comfort zone and beyond which she or he may have blind spots. A narrow range indicates a lack of flexibility and understanding of other approaches, whereas a wide range indicates the opposite.

However, in most cases the development of style-shifting will require working with a coach over a period of time, and preferably embedded in the specific leadership and negotiation contexts to build this skill effectively.

Cultural dialogue: This is the ability to engage stakeholders in an exploration of their differences in order to negotiate mutual adaptations and alignment. This is a form of meta-negotiation upon which the success of the nominal negotiation can critically depend. Cultural dialogue requires facilitation skills that are informed by adequate cultural due diligence and perspective taking. It is particularly recommended when it is not clear or cannot be assumed which stakeholder readily assumes the responsibility to adapt to the other or where the pressure to adapt creates experiences that generate resentments and/or resistance, which can easily undermine a given undertaking. This is particularly relevant for highly diverse and heterogeneous teams that need to establish norms that enable effective team-work and collaboration.

Cultural mentoring: This is the proactive use of cultural insights and understanding to help others navigate them effectively, so that they can become effective participants in the cultural context. Cultural mentoring makes the implicit (unwritten rules, expectations, and norms) explicit and therefore accessible to those unfamiliar with them. As such, it is integral to effective on-boarding and integration into a new culture and/or con-text and creates the conditions for effective transactions, interactions, and relationships.

Cultural mentoring in particular is also critical to relieve the awkward tension and discomfort that often accompanies intercultural differences and the ambiguity and uncertainty they create. This is also where humor and playfulness can play an important role, because of their humanizing effect, as discussed in Chapter 1. Particularly when style differences create mixed sig-nals, miscommunication, judgments, and intolerance about others, they can powerfully—and as shown in Chapter 1—memorably release and transform tension. The following case illustrates this effect.

At S. Marten Company's last senior leadership team meeting, Benjamin took several minutes to introduce the newest member, Kim Park, to the group.

Benjamin said, "I expect and reward 'telling it like it is' . . . we value speaking up here if we disagree. Isn't that right, Charlotte?"

Charlotte noticed Kim's face as if he had a question mark on his forehead as she tried to explain what Benjamin meant.

Charlotte stumbled, "Yes, that's correct, Benjamin, you like to be direct and reinforce this kind of communication in our team. That is correct."

"Mr. Park," Benjamin emphasized, "we value open discussion and resolution of all disagreements in our discussions. We handle them in an impersonal and objective way. We always get quick results this way."

"Conflict is positive and constructive here even when tensions are high," concluded Benjamin. "We are honest and trustworthy here—full transparency . . . we love it."

As Charlotte observed the room, she noticed a shock of resentment and annoyance rise deep from inside. She was getting tired of what she felt was

"Benjamin's endless embarrassing, insulting, insensitive, and incompetent" way of representing the leadership team to their first Asian member.

In her earlier conversations with Kim, she sensed that he had a less critical and challenging attitude about differences. Charlotte was excited to get some new ideas and practical perspective about the growth in their South Korean markets. She felt fatigued and even depressed that Benjamin's open conflict approach in their leadership meetings would squeeze out Kim's more "civil" and sensitive tone.

Charlotte surprised herself when she blurted out, "Don't worry Kim. We DO have some emotional and social intelligence in this team . . . Benjamin's just negative. The rest of us have a sense of dignity and integrity and don't need to openly display our disturbing thoughts."

Benjamin jumped in, "Kim, you don't have to worry that we're all weak, evasive, and suspicious about what we want around here . . . . Charlotte, is a minority."

"What?" Charlotte exclaimed as she stood up from her chair and walked toward the door . . . the room fell silent.

Charlotte closed her eyes as she stopped with her hand on the door, and felt her shoulders drop. She took a deep breath, and began to laugh as she turned around to look at Benjamin's ashen face. She laughed again and said they should all take a deep breath. "Where did all this come from?" she exclaimed. "This really is a playful competition, but I forget that, like today!"

"I'm sorry, I'm trying so hard to be less anxious about expressing our concerns in such a public way," Charlotte said. "This is crazy and we don't mean any of this." You are really the most good-natured person I know . . . and you know how to get me into a frenzy."

Benjamin chuckled, "I have been trying to watch myself with this directness and 'skipped the curb'—I know how annoyed I am about avoiding our disagreements. It's hilarious how we clash on this so often—even while trying not to be so thoughtless. I am actually working on not being too critical in our meetings and I don't want to embarrass anyone. I really don't. Charlotte, catch me on it quicker and we can figure out the best way to respect our approaches."

Charlotte said, "Next time I won't storm out, but will pull my scarf over my head to remind you, Benjamin, that I'm uncomfortable with your directness. Welcome, Kim, to our creative leadership circle playground, unleashing creativity has never been more fun . . . ."

Kim exclaimed, "I will never forget this introduction and your commitment to real innovation and energy."

When colleagues like Charlotte and Benjamin have disagreements they are uptight and too goal focused, which can stifle trust building, team collaboration, and true partnering. Playfulness helps bring about a conducive, collaborative, and relaxed state of mind that creates a powerful social foundation.

Summary

Just like quantum physics is the science of the invisible (and surprising) aspects and forces that make up reality, Quantum Negotiation (and Quantum Leadership) entails being alert and attentive to the seemingly small and invisible aspects that underpin human thinking, feeling, and behavior. There is much for Quantum Leaders to apply from the emerging insights of neuroscience and the connections between the social, psychological, cultural, and emotional aspects of human behavior. The Quantum approach integrates what we know about negotiation with knowledge of intercultural dimensions and neuroscience.

The Quantum Negotiation Profile offers a practical framework for discovery, awareness building, and skill development as part of the essential preparation. It is a tool that provides insights that help us support individuals in their development of quantum skills, encouraging them to become active observers of others and to develop behaviors and skills that are inclusive when working with individuals with differing approaches. The strategic skills and capabilities of cultural due diligence, frame shifting, style-shifting, cultural dialogue, and cultural mentoring can be developed and supported by the Quantum Negotiation Profile in practical and tangible ways.

6 | Leading Is Not about the Leader

Do you remember Lina from the introduction? She was the discouraged project manager who was entrusted to spearhead the development of a new values statement for her multinational organization. This venture was part of a CEO-driven transformation to a purpose-driven and values-led organization. The strong resistance and antagonistic attitudes in the organization did not bode well for success. Lina was discouraged, but not deterred. She understood that she needed a savvy approach. She recognized clearly that her success rested on her ability to negotiate agreements, endorsements, and support for a change that nobody wanted and many openly resisted. She reflected deeply on the mission on which she was about to embark. Carefully assessing the situation, she drew three key conclusions that would transform the way she approached her mission:

1. The resistance she encountered was in fact a positive sign of attachment to a values foundation that was profoundly admirable. After all, she knew from friends in other organizations that corporate values were often little more than wall decoration.

2. For this project to be successful, employees, and particularly leaders in the organization, could a get a sense of "internal colonialism" or "headquarter imposition." The symbolic power struggle that this could create would undermine the eventual success of this project.

3. The pride of ownership of these values was exactly what the CEO wanted to tap into with his transformation to a purpose-led and values-driven approach. But, this was not about *new* values that he needed, but a better, more contemporary and appealing *articulation* of what leaders in the organization already valued, cared about, and protected.

On the basis of these conclusions, she reframed her entire approach. She embarked on a series of conversations with influential leaders (both in titled leadership positions and within informal networks) across the international footprint of the organization, focusing on the United States, where there was the most resistance. The purpose of these conversations was to create a personal context in which she could communicate that this was not an abandonment, but rather a rearticulation of the company's values in more compelling terms. She wanted to understand what these leaders actually valued, so that those values would be reflected in the resulting articulation.

She did not have any experience doing this and was particularly apprehensive of talking with angry, dismissive, and hard-nosed executives. Lina used deliberate techniques to help her remain grounded and focused, enabling her to show up with empathy, curiosity, and openness.

The conversations went well, and helped her created a sense among the leaders that (1) this would not be a dreaded imposition by headquarters, (2) the output could be something that reflected them, (3) they had input in crafting it, and (4) it would reflect a deep and thorough understanding of what drives them in their work.

Over a series of several months and investment into repeated conversations, she managed to turn the energy of resistance into an energy of support. The transparency she created about her process also gave these leaders a sense of control, which was important as they were used to headquarters undermining their sense of control on key issues.

Lina meticulously documented the content of what was shared in these conversations, extracting common themes and language, and interpreting the stories of prideful success in a highly open and transparent process for everyone. She socialized various wording options, and cycled them between a small workgroup of formal leaders from each business unit that the CEO had created to serve as a sounding board for Lina's work and the participants in her conversations.

With each turn, the relationship and trust she built and the respect she showed helped her maintain the integrity of her process. When, in the end, the new articulation of the values was formally announced, no one was surprised, turned off, or unsupportive. The smooth adoption of the new articulation was even a surprise to many leaders themselves. To this day, this project ranks among the most successful change leadership projects across the organization.

Lina learned a lot about leadership through this experience. As a result of her success, she gained a reputation for being able to make the improbable real, and she has been entrusted with other difficult change projects since then. Lina has made the Quantum mindset a hallmark of her overall approach to change leadership.

In chapters 4 and 5, we identified interdependence and the subtle, largely invisible forces in human behavior as foundational to the Quantum mindset. The implication is that *inter*dependence is not an objective state, but an active and deliberate *practice* and that it is anchored by an alignment of attitudes and intentions—what we pay attention to and how we engage and influence social processes. All these need to be guided by the sincere and credible pursuit of mutual gains and sustainable benefits for all stakeholders. Both our attitudes and intentions need each other, for our attitudes are swayed and subjected to the invisible forces discussed earlier and can easily be abused in the services of exploitative self-interest. It is only when we pair our attention with the intention and attitude of mutuality that we achieve sustainable value.

Leaders are negotiating whenever there is something that they need from someone else. That may be with an executive from a different organization, an administrative assistant, a colleague, or a family member. Leaders need followership in order to achieve their collective goals and can rarely achieve said goals without directly negotiating with their followers.

Leaders engage in implicit negotiation on a daily basis—as we discuss where we would like to eat as a group, request that someone give a presentation, or persuade colleagues to support our decisions. We tend to value leaders who succeed at explicit negotiation more than leaders who consistently negotiate implicitly.

Quantum Leadership Resonance and Mindfulness

Wendy Asks:

What can I do to make sure I am having compassion and understanding while still maintaining a position of power or authority?

Quantum Negotiation skills are required in leadership at all levels in today's era of incivility, disruption, and accelerating speed. With a focus on personal growth, Quantum Negotiators expand their view to support the larger collective to navigate new opportunities, create new resources, and accelerate sustainable social change together. With intention and attention to practice Quantum Negotiation skills, their personal growth and life experiences inspire families, colleagues, organizations, and teams in new ways. There is a magnetism or contagion of engagement and clarity about individual and collective motivation to ask questions, cocreate, share resources, solve problems—the art of getting needs met.

Quantum Leaders are mindful to manage their own emotions, recognize others' stress, practice civility, ask questions, recognize others' manipulative tactics, and share information. The less they act from a defensive and dominating position, the more positive their influence will be with others, and the more positive will be the overall experience of both work and personal aspects of their lives. If you observe current leaders in organizations, chances are good that you will find some leaders who encourage us-versus-them attitudes, practice silo behavior, and make selfish decisions.

For example, we worked with an organization that had a variety of function leaders in, for example, legal, human resources, and finance. These departments regularly placed stops in each other's way. Human resources would request something from legal and legal would reject the request. Legal would then need someone from the finance department to go over their budget, but finance would fail to make anyone from their department available, and when finance needed reports from human resources, human resources refused to send them the reports. This destructive ripple effect put the entire organization in a headlock. Only after these function leaders took the time to negotiate with one another did the organization start to run like a well-oiled machine.

Thomas Asks:

What did that organization's leaders do in order to get to the point where they could all negotiate?

As Quantum Leaders develop, they recognize that they need to understand themselves and their counterparts. After that is accomplished, they often recognize their insecurities about negotiating and can engage with their counterparts in healthy ways.

Quantum Leader preparation for reflection, awareness, and flexibility before negotiating with others has both cognitive and physical implications for followership and leadership. When the mind and body come under stress in conflict situations or by manipulation habits of others, Quantum Leaders explore the unseen disruption to their own nervous system and prepare to anchor themselves so they can create a resonance of psychological safety for others.

When Quantum Negotiators are attacked, or manipulated in a negotiation, the choice to anchor oneself and acknowledge the potential for attack is a critical first step in successful dialogue. Anchoring is a psychological experience when mind, body, and spirit become fully integrated because it creates a balance, connection, and awareness of a relationship between one's self and others in a negotiation . . . much like the anchor to the buoy under turbulent, disturbing waters.

Some Quantum Negotiators use Aikido or other practices that are founded on the knowledge of anchoring as an internal sensory and calming practice, which enhances a contagion of safety in a conflict group. Much of the tactical training in classic Machiavellian negotiation asserts that it is necessary to concentrate forces to destroy and weaken the will of a counterpart. The key to leadership in this coercive strategy is a single-mindedness of purpose and absolute concentration on the sole task: to win at all costs.

This approach can be used successfully because Machiavellian negotiators believe most people live in a "state of distraction, and thus, a focused arrow will find its mark every time because it is easy to overwhelm and beat the distracted into submission." Aggressive and attacking behavior, intimidation, the nibble, take-it-or-leave it, highball or lowball offers, and snow jobs are some examples used by such hardball leaders. Quantum Negotiators do not respond in kind, however; they change the game because of the risk to reputation, lost deals, relationships, futility, and sense of integrity.

Quantum Negotiators find that there are very few agreements that are a single transaction and that the relationship is important. Therefore, they prepare to engage and foster the working relationships by increasing their psychological and strategic advantage to change the game and NOT play the Machiavellian game. Several Quantum Leaders in the military compare Quantum Practices to the insights from Mindfulness-based Mind Fitness Training (MMFT), Mindfit, and Warrior Mind Training, for example. These practices are based on findings in neuroscience, security, and human performance research that have implications for stressful negotiation situations. For Quantum Negotiators, hardball attempts to lead in a destructive situation are extremely stressful and can weaken their clear decision-making performance.

Ordering versus Engaging

Wendy Asks:

Controlling is really easy for me to default into. What do you suggest I do to better engage with employees like Lina, without hurting my image or losing important time for other work?

Over the past five years, "Jose's" company rapidly expanded its products through several acquisitions in Latin America, Europe, and Asia. Jose has been his company's lead negotiator to align his own team of global sales, operations, and consumer services across several time zones.

Just before a coaching session recently, Jose became "unhinged" by the lack of cooperation and lack of energy in his own team. He had been working with them for months to agree on a strategy for an upcoming meeting with a new partner in Latin America.

Jose used the coaching session to explore why he was so frustrated and asked, "Why is all the work I've done for months not appreciated by my team? Who is going to step up and help me get something done?"

He felt he deserved the team's collaboration and that he was not being treated fairly in their interactions. Jose realized how angry, impatient, cynical, and resentful he was about his colleagues but did not know what to do.

Jose faced a dilemma. Was the problem his leadership OR his colleagues' lack of motivation? What should he focus his attention on? What Jose realized was that it is the paradox of BOTH. Because Jose has a genuine interest in developing his leadership impact, he reflected on his own leadership first.

One of his tendencies is to react as a leader with an attitude of entitlement and justice. When he is stressed, he becomes reactive and persuades others to pay attention to what he thinks is important and he wants to be recognized and valued. He is focusing on himself rather than taking the time to remember to include and recognize others' contributions.

He also realized that he did not provide enough time to engage his colleagues. This, he believed, dampened their motivation to collaborate with him. As he reviewed his leadership of the negotiation process, he realized that he focused primarily on what he believed was the common ground, but did not fully listen or appreciate what others were paying attention to.

Preparation for his next team meeting and calls required Jose to be more aware of his own experience of feelings and thoughts, to share them, and engage the team to do the same. With some team members, he needed to acknowledge and even readdress some of the past ideas and concerns that he rejected. He needed to establish a level of commitment by the team and to continually check for common understanding.

With practice, Jose has committed to his own leadership development by mobilizing his own energy and enthusiasm to learn. He catches himself when he feels entitled to other's cooperation. He has received positive feedback from his colleagues that his eagerness and sense of responsibility to effectively lead the team has been noticed. With a shift in attention from Jose's own need for recognition to the best interests of the team relationship, his colleagues' motivation and energy began to change as well.

Quantum Negotiators utilize "mindfulness" as a process of bringing one's attention to the present experience on a moment-by-moment basis and in a nonjudgmental way. Mindfulness differs from a cognitive mode of processing information or thinking. In other words, paying attention is not the same thing as thinking, although the two are often equated. These are like the Quantum Negotiation anchoring practices that support the efficacy of mindfulness-based interventions, such as focus exercises and meditation.

There are many neuroscience studies that conclude that, as a result, there is an improvement in physical and psychological resilience, attention, immune functioning, mood, and sense of well-being, in addition to increased tolerance for difficult situations.

It has long been believed that stress is due to external events that degrade performance. However, stress is now defined as a perceived, internal condition. The right amount of stress will allow a Quantum Negotiator to function at peak performance. However, excessive perceived stress has biological and psychological consequences that reduce the capacity to process new information and learn. Stress may also bias negotiators more toward reactive, unconscious defensive choices.

Quantum Negotiation preparation is like Mind Fitness Training and Performance Optimal programs, which prepare for capacities of mental agility, emotional regulation, attention, and situational awareness (of self, others, and the wider environment). Just as physical fitness corresponds to specific enhancements in the body, mind fitness practices are prominent in high-performance negotiation preparation. Neuroscience research asserts that enhancements in specific brain structures and functions support high-performance capacities in that they build resiliency and lead to faster recovery from cognitive depletion and psychological stress. Preparation can improve self-regulation, adaptation, and attention skills, and enhance situational awareness and agility.

Based on the neuroscience work about the neuroplasticity of the brain and inoculation from the world of medicine, the introduction of a stressful situation through training can "vaccinate" Quantum Negotiators and increase their resilience against stress and hardball negotiation attacks. Quantum Leaders build confidence to lead and follow, set goals, and channel energy under stress through anchoring themselves and engaging with others.

These practices increase Quantum Leaders' abilities to change the hardball negotiation games and to create resonance and psychological safety in teams and relationships. Some practices include asking to come back to conflicting issues later, listening for critical clues, or asking others for advice or support. In addition, these mindfulness practices help Quantum Leaders recognize when they may be difficult to negotiate with themselves. Most importantly, mindfulness practices inoculate Quantum Leaders from driving a larger wedge between themselves and their original negotiation goals, purpose, and integrity.

Yvonne's Mindful Leadership and Civility

> ## Thomas Asks:
>
> What can I do to prepare for my daily negotiations?

Yvonne was a headhunter for a global recruitment firm that had many demanding clients searching for top global talent, especially in Latin America. She professionally screened candidates for clients. However, some clients spoke to her very harshly and were dismissive of what she presented to them, ranging from salary and school expectations all the way to cultural fit and hobbies.

Despite practicing her Quantum Negotiation skills in problem solving with them, it was difficult for Yvonne to find what would make them happy or what solution they could come up with together. At these times, she would first feel paralyzed, impatient, and apologetic because of their controlling behavior. And as time went on, she would get very defensive and harsh in her own behavior. She recalls a time she shouted at the client, "Do the search yourself!" This was not the professional and civil behavior she intended for herself.

Yvonne learned that not only did she need to practice mindfulness prior to meeting with clients, but she also had to anchor herself on the spot and in the moment. She found that not only did she need to pay attention to her presentations, but also to her emotional frustration, physical exhaustion, and sense of purpose when negotiating with clients. Overall, she has learned to be more confident in her ability to remain diplomatic and conciliatory with even the most coercive clients. Yvonne knows that executive searches are subjective and rarely conclude in complete satisfaction. She knows that using her feelings and intuitions to know the right needs and fit in many situations is part of the art.

Rather than doubt herself and her skills when she negotiates with hardball clients, she now practices her anchoring and breathing exercises to calm her nervous system. Yvonne has experienced a sense of satisfaction about her own behavior and has noticed how the game changes with hardball clients to be more conciliatory because she sets the tone.

Summary: *Leading Is Not about the Leader*

In a time of exponential change and disruption, new rules are emerging: from leadership as a dominating, controlling, authoritative commander to a master negotiator of engagement and transformation. On a global scale, people are thinking, acting, relating, and purchasing in entirely new ways. There is a disruption to old-school business and negotiation norms of control and domination from the past. The constant disruption and speed of change are destabilizing predictable pathways to personal and organizational leadership effectiveness and satisfaction. Discoveries in neuroscience provide important information about how to keep our brains more elastic and adaptable to keep pace.

Quantum Leaders are learning to unlearn or let go of outmoded beliefs and to embrace principles that will positively multiply or accelerate collective engagement to create new opportunities. Limited negotiation success, and stress associated with old ways of coping with control, lead to elevated cortisol levels that hamper synaptic connections and brain function for individuals and groups. Those leaders who can consciously move beyond beliefs about control and switch to positive approaches and engagement with others can perform and innovate more rapidly.

As the circle of attention from egoism to sociocentrism and shared interests expands, Quantum Leaders anchor with full attention and presence to connect and lead in a widening sphere of social experiences. By slowing down, a quantum space opens and there is a stronger and more heightened connection with the world around them. Quantum Leaders invest in their own personal resilience and optimism to take a wider perspective to see connections and the needs of others around them. They practice the art of getting what they need while inspiring and accelerating the capacity for others to do the same.

As Alvin Toffler predicted, "The illiterate of the 21st century will not be those who can't read and write, but those who cannot learn, unlearn and relearn."

Conclusion

Do you remember Paula and Martin, whose dilemmas were showcased in the introduction? Both reflect real negotiators confronted with difficult situations. They could achieve what they needed by methodologically applying the insights and practices of our Quantum approach.

Paula's aggressive, hardball negotiation strategy with the wholesale "Goliath" had led to a stalemate that culminated in a disastrous two-hour meeting. That meeting left Paula and Ben, the buyer, exasperated; and Paula was in a panic from seeing this deal, one that could make or break her career, in jeopardy.

It took this moment of crisis to make her step back and evaluate her role in creating this dilemma. Explicit situations carry this risk of becoming so locked in to our goals and approach that we lose perspective. A significant crisis or an experience of near failure can be exactly what we need to regain perspective, understand the quantum variables involved, redirect our actions, reset the relationship, and thereby restore the chances of success.

Paula was able to transform her approach to this more virtuous cycle. She approached Ben's context, specifically the retail supply chain, with new openness and curiosity. She also discovered how anxious she had been and how her fear of failure and perception of risk and scarcity of options drove her aggressiveness toward Ben. This was aggravated by a prevailing norm in her own organization where overachieving aggressive goals was a badge of honor. In a male-dominated environment, she felt extra pressure to perform and prove her value. Paula realized that her zeal and independent ego-orientation kept her from thinking more clearly about their shared interests.

She took time to clear her head and rest. Upon reflection, she did not like the way she must have come across to Ben. Calming down her own nervous system enabled her to establish clarity and become grounded in a completely different approach. Paula apologized for her behavior and began to ask Ben more questions about his needs. She explored ways they could creatively save money in his complex supply network, and soon she and Ben agreed upon a new comanagement supplier agreement not only around shoes, but also other items. They found a new way to manage the inventory levels and ways they could help customers pay even less. In the end, both Paula and Ben could improve their margins.

Besides learning about herself, Paula also realized that an aggressive focus on price inevitably ends in deadlock. She already knew this in theory, but she surprised herself by how quickly she got into a bidding war with Ben. She learned not to put price as the centerpiece, but to invest more time in developing a relationship with Ben and to support him in mutual gains. When she remembered to think in terms of a partnership and focus on a common goal, such as cutting costs, she could engage with Ben in developing long-term, mutually beneficial solutions.

She also began to see Ben as another ambitious professional who wanted to do well and who needed to navigate a complex organization. Creating a relationship of mutual understanding of one another's intentions and qualifications, they created a mutually supportive and trusting relationship. Surprisingly, forging this relationship also helped eliminate elaborate legal contracts; they used letters of intent and established joint problem-solving and information-sharing processes to quickly meet both of their needs.

In hindsight, both Paula and Ben were amazed at her transformation, the relatively short time in which it came about, and the results they achieved, even when it had seemed out of reach so early on in their relationship. Paula frequently says, "Without having run into this wall, I would have never seriously believed that paying attention to seemingly small aspects of my own internal experience, attitudes, and assumptions could unlock such a profoundly positive shift!" Since then, she has become an enthusiastic Quantum Negotiator.

★ ★ ★

Martin's story is similar in many aspects, yet different in the context and specifics. Most significantly, his sense of profound crisis provided the impetus to regain perspective, better understand his quantum reality and the choices available to him, redirect actions, reset the relationships involved, and thereby restore both their chances of success. You may recall from the introduction that Martin did not get anywhere in the negotiations with Renaldo on the acquisition of WINSOME. He felt like he was failing an important test of his leadership capabilities. This experience confirmed a deeply held belief that, as an accountant, he was just not a good negotiator.

Keeping his self-doubt well hidden, Martin called for a recess in the negotiations. He reflected deeply on his experience and came to understand that conflict with Renaldo was not bad or dysfunctional. He realized how much his deep-seated conflict adversity contributed to the difficulties he experienced. Resetting and realigning his own emotional and spiritual needs would help him cooperate with Renaldo and not get flustered by Renaldo's aggressive style. Martin also cleared his thinking and focused on the business problem that needed to be fixed—the purchase price was too high because of obvious financial discrepancies.

Martin planned for a mutual-gains strategy by asking Renaldo to explore how they both could come up with a solution. Martin focused on the common problems they had and told Renaldo he was willing to preserve a relationship, but that Renaldo needed to explore the consequences of the misaligned financial systems. By anchoring his own needs and taking a long-term, strategic focus, Martin was able to engage Renaldo in a more flexible attitude and shared responsibility for the adjustment in price.

With a focus on their interdependent and mutual needs to get this deal done, and maintaining his internal alignment, Martin was able to problem solve with Renaldo for a resolution. Not only did they find a way to reduce the purchase price, but they were also able to create a more centralized coordination of transactions to expedite the global due diligence process. Martin also learned to appreciate that what he experienced first as an aggressive stance by Renaldo was in fact a more emotionally engaged and direct communication style that had simply clashed with his preferred style of indirectness.

With greater understanding, appreciation, and cooperation, he learned where to look and what to look for to identify significant inaccuracies in the financial reporting, including the misplaced reporting codes. Martin was happy to report to the board that he not only got a purchase price reduction, but also found a way to reduce the central costs and loss of purchasing synergies for the new enterprise going forward.

Martin was proud of himself on the day he sat in his new chair as the CFO of the newly acquired organization! He had proven, most of all to himself, that accountants can be good Quantum Negotiators. To this day, he attributes his career success to the personal and professional growth he derived from taking a quantum perspective. The nonjudgmental perspective of style differences in particular has left a lasting impression, and he has become a great champion and coach who helps others develop and apply the ability to style-shift.

Both Paula and Martin have been transformed through the spark of a perceived crisis. Instead of doubling down on their approach or opting out altogether, they leaned into this transformational opportunity and did not dismiss the focus on the seemingly small and unperceivable aspects, the quanta, that have an impact on the negotiation process and prospective outcomes.

Paula and Martin were each led to the point of regaining perspective, redirecting actions with intention and alignment, purposefully resetting relationships, and restoring or enhancing their chances of success. The results they achieved were a surprise to them and their stakeholders. And that is, in fact, the essential value proposition of the quantum approach—the tapping of unexpected value and the achievement of surprising outcomes. This is accomplished through a shift in our understanding and focus, and the alignment of the five essential elements of human action and interaction—the physical, cognitive, behavioral, emotional, and spiritual.

And this is where we leave this exploration of Quantum Negotiation. We hope that one thing has become particularly clear, namely that Quantum Negotiation is not simply another set of techniques and tactics to enhance your negotiation toolkit; rather, Quantum Negotiation is a different way of being, preparing for, and showing up across the multitude of implicit or explicit negotiations. It is an inward journey through deeply held assumptions, beliefs, attitudes, and aspirations that helps you to be and remain anchored at the center, so that you can be flexible in your responses. The more complex, ambiguous, and unpredictable our environment becomes, the more essential is the mindset and practice of Quantum Negotiation.

QN References and Further Reading

QN Introduction

Covey, Stephen R. and Rebecca R. Merrill. *The Speed of Trust: The One Thing That Ehanges Everything.* New York: Simon & Schuster, 2008.

Swart, Tara, Kitty Chisholm, and Paul Brown. *Neuroscience for Leadership.* London: Palgrave, 2015.

PART I
QN Chapter 1

Babcock, Linda, and Sara Laschever. *Women Don't Ask: The High Cost of Avoiding Negotiation—And Positive Strategies for Change.* New York: Bantam Books, 2007.

Bos, Maarten, "The Unconscious Executive." *HBR Working Knowledge Newsletter* (July 9, 2012). http://hbswk.hbs.edu/item/the-unconscious-executive

Cain, Susan. *Quiet: The Power of Introverts in a World That Can't Stop Talking.* New York: Crown, 2012.

Capra, Fritjof. *The Web of Life: New Scientific Understanding of Living Systems.* New York: Anchor Books, 1997.

Chira, Susan. "The Universal Phenomenon of Men Interrupting Women." *New York Times* (June 14, 2017). https://www.nytimes.com/2017/06/14/business/women-sexism-work-huffington-kamala-harris.html?_r=0

Coleman, Isobel. "The Global Glass Ceiling: Why Empowering Women Is Good for Business." *Foreign Affairs* 89, no. 3 (May/June, 2010). https://www.foreignaffairs.com/articles/2010-05-01/global-glass-ceiling

De Koven, Bernard. "Playfulness Is a Spiritual Practice." *Psychology Today.* https://www.psychologytoday.com/blog/having-fun/201511/playfulness-is-spiritual-practice

Fritz, H. L., L. N. Russek, and M. M., Dillon. "Humor Use Moderates the Relation of Stressful Life Events with Psychological Distress." *Personality and Social Psychology Bulletin* 43 no. 6 (2017): 845-859.

George, B., P. Sim, A. McLean, and D. Mayer. "Discovering Your Authentic Leadership." *Harvard Business Review* 87, no. 2 (February 2007): 129–138.

Hagerty, Barbara Bradley. *Fingerprints of God: The Search for the Science of Spirituality*. New York: Riverhead Books, 2009.

Hardt, James V. *The Art of Smart Thinking: Treat Yourself to a Brain Make-Over*. Santa Clara, CA: Biocybernaut Press, 2007.

Hicks, Donna. *Dignity: The Essential Role It Plays in Resolving Conflict*. New Haven, CT: Yale University Press, 2011.

Kanter, Rosabeth Moss. "Manage Yourself: Zoom In, Zoom Out." *Harvard Business Review* 89, no. 3 March 2011. https://hbr.org/2011/03/managing-yourself-zoom-in-zoom-out

Krakovsky, Marina. "Mixed Impressions: How We Judge Others on Multiple Levels." *Scientific American*, (January 28, 2010). https://www.scientificamerican.com/search/?q=Mixed+Impressions%3A+How+We+Judge+Others+on+Multiple+Levels

Lehrer, Jonah. *How We Decide*. Boston: Mariner Books, 2010.

Medina, John. *Brain Rules: 12 Principles for Surviving and Thriving at Work, Home, and School*. Seattle: Pear Press, 2009.

Newberg, Andrew, and Mark Robert Waldman. *How God Changes Your Brain: Breakthrough Findings from a Neuroscientist*. New York: Ballantine Books, 2009.

Peltin, Scott, and Jogi Rippel. *Sink, Float, or Swim: Sustainable High Performance Doesn't Happen by Chance—It Happens by Choice*. Munich: Redline, 2009.

Scharmer, Otto, and Katrin Kaufer. *Leading from the Emerging Future: From Ego-System to Eco-System Economies*. New York: Berrett-Koehler, 2013.

Solnit, Rebecca. *Men Explain Things to Me*. New York: Haymarket Books, 2014.

Yale Center for Faith and Culture. "Spiritual Capital Initiative." Yale University. 2012. http://spiritualcapital.yale.edu

Walch, Karen. *The Power of Understanding*. Boston: Acanthus 2013.

QN Chapter 2

Amen, Daniel G. *Change Your Brain, Change Your Life: The Breakthrough Programme for Conquering Anger, Anxiety and Depression*. London: Piatkus Books, 2009.

Brooks, David. *The Road to Character*. New York: Random House, 2015.

Carney, Dana, Amy Cuddy, and Andy Yap. "Power Posing: Brief Non-verbal Displays Affect Neuroendocrine Levels and Risk Tolerance." *Psychological Science* 21, no. 10 (October 2010): 1363–1368

Fisher, Roger, and William Ury. *Getting to Yes*. New York: Penguin, 1981.

Fisher, Roger, and Daniel Shapiro. *Beyond Reason: Using Emotions as You Negotiate*. New York: Viking, 2006.

Goleman, Daniel. *Brain and Emotional Intelligence: New Insights*. Northampton, MA: More Than Sound, 2011.

Kegan, Robert, and Lisa Laskow. *Immunity to Change: How to Overcome It and Unlock the Potential in Yourself and Your Organization*. Cambridge, MA: Harvard Business Review Press, 2009

Pink, Daniel H. *Drive: The Surprising Truth About What Motivates Us*. New York: Riverhead Books, 2009.

Seligman, Martin E.P. *Learned Optimism: How to Change Your Mind and Your Life*. New York: Pocket Books, 2006.

Sinek, Simon. *Start with Why: How Great Leaders Inspire Everyone to Take Action*. New York: Portfolio, 2009.

Ury, William. *The Power of a Positive No: How to Say No and Still Get to Yes*. New York: Bantam Books, 2007.

QN Chapter 3

Cuddy, Amy. *Presence: Bringing Your Boldest Self to Your Biggest Challenges*. New York: Little, Brown, 2015

Evans, Patricia. *Controlling People: How to Recognize, Understand, and Deal with People Who Try to Control You.* Avon, MA: Adams Media, 2002.

Goleman, Daniel. *Social Intelligence: The New Science of Human Relationships.* New York: Bantam Dell, 2006.

Goleman, Daniel. *Brain and Emotional Intelligence: New Insights.* Northampton, MA: More Than Sound, 2011.

Greene, Robert, and Joost Elffers. *The 48 Laws of Power.* New York: Penguin, 2000.

Malhotra, Deepak, and Max H. Bazerman. *Negotiation Genius: How to Overcome Obstacles and Achieve Brilliant Results at the Bargaining Table and Beyond.* New York: Bantam Books, 2007.

Menkel-Meadow, Carrie, and Michael Wheeler. *What's Fair: Ethics for Negotiation.* San Francisco: Jossey-Bass, 2004.

Shell, G. Richard. *Bargaining for Advantage: Negotiation Strategies for Reasonable People.* New York: Penguin Books, 2008.

Wheeler, Michael. *The Art of Negotiation: How to Improvise Agreement in a Chaotic World.* New York: Simon and Schuster, 2013.

PART II

Lewicki, Roy J., David M. Saunders, and Bruce Barry. *Essentials of Negotiation.* New York: McGraw- Hill, 2011.

PART III

QN Chapter 4

Diamandis, Peter H. and Steven Kotler. *Abundance: The Future Is Better Than You Think.* New York: Simon and Schuster, 2012.

Diamandis, Peter H. *Bold: How to Go Big, Create Wealth and Impact the World.* New York: Simon and Schuster, 2015.

Colvile, Robert. *The Great Acceleration: How the World Is Getting Faster, Faster.* New York: Bloomsbury, 2016.

Friedman, Thomas L. *Thank You for Being Late: An Optimist's Guide to Thriving in the Age of Accelerations.* New York: Macmillan, 2016.

Horney, N., B. Pasmore, and T. O'Shea. "Leadership Agility: A Business Imperative for a VUCA World." *People and Strategy* 33, no. 4 (2010). http://leadership-agility.net/uncategorized/leadership-agility-a-business-imperative-for-a-vuca-world/

Khanna, Parag. *Connectography: Mapping the Future of Global Civilization.* New York: Random House, 2016.

Schwab, Klaus. *The Fourth Industrial Revolution.* London: Crown Publishing, 2017.

QN Chapter 5

Brynjolfsson, Erik, and Andrew McAfee. *The Second Machine Age: Work, Progress, and Prosperity in a Time of Brilliant Technologies.* New York: W.W. Norton, 2014.

Dinkin, Steve, Barbara Filner, and Lisa Maxwell. *The Exchange: A Bold and Proven Approach to Resolving Workplace Conflict.* Portland, OR: Productivity Press, 2011.

Ghemawat, Pankaj. "Globalization in the Age of Trump." *Harvard Business Review* (July–August 2017): 112–123. https://hbr.org/2017/07/globalization-in-the-age-of-trump

Ismail, Salim, and Michael S. Malone. *Exponential Organizations: Why New Organizations Are Ten Times Better, Faster, and Cheaper Than Yours (And What to Do About It).* New York: Diversion Books, 2014.

Johnson Vicberg, Suzanne M., and Kim Christfort. "Pioneers, Drivers, Integrators and Guardians." *Harvard Business Review* (March–April 2017): 50–61. https://hbr.org/2017/03/the-new-science-of-team-chemistry#pioneers-drivers-integrators-and-guardians

Kegan, Robert, Lisa Laskow Lahey, and Matthew L Miller. *An Everyone Culture: Becoming a Deliberately Developmental Organization.* Cambridge, MA: Harvard Business Review Press, 2016.

Kets de Vries, Manfred F. R. "Managing Yourself: Do You Hate Your Boss." *Harvard Business Review* (December 2016): 98–101. https://hbr.org/search?search_type=search-all&term=Managing+Yourself%3A+++Do+you+You+Hate+Your+Boss

National Research Council. *Emerging Cognitive Neuroscience and Related Technologies.* Washington, DC: The National Academies Press, 2008.

Putz, Lynne Elaine, Joerg Schmitz, and Karen Walch. *Maximizing Business Results with the Strategic Performance Framework.* Saline, MI: McNaughton & Gunn, 2014.

QN Chapter 6

Ancona, Deborah, Thomas W. Malone, Wanda J. Orlikowski, and Peter M. Senge. "In Praise of the Incomplete Leader." Harvard Business Review (February 2007): 92–100.

Bos, Maarten, "The Unconscious Executive." *HBR Working Knowledge Newsletter* (July 9, 2012). http://hbswk.hbs.edu/item/the-unconscious-executive

Bossons, Patricia, Patricia Riddell, and Denis Sartain. *The Neuroscience of Leadership Coaching: Why the Tools and Techniques of Leadership Coaching Work.* London: Bloomsbury Books, 2015.

Brown, Brene. *Rising Strong.* New York: Random House, 2015.

Fisher, Roger, and Daniel Shapiro. *Beyond Reason: Using Emotions as You Negotiate.* New York: Viking, 2006.

Gratton, Lynda, and Andrew Scott. *The 100-Year Life: Living and Working in an Age of Longevity.* London: Bloomsbury, 2016.

Greene, Robert, and Joost Elffers. *The 48 Laws of Power.* New York: Penguin, 2000.

Kahneman, D. *Thinking, Fast and Slow.* New York: Farrar, Straus and Giroux, 2011.

Pearson, Christine, and Christine Lynne Povath. *The Cost of Bad Behavior: How Incivility Is Damaging Your Business and What to Do about It.* New York: Penguin, 2009.

Scharmer, C. Otto. *Theory U: Leading from the Future as It Emerges.* New York: Berrett-Koehler, 2016.

Sinek, Simon. *Leaders Eat Last: Why Some Teams Pull Together and Others Don't.* New York: Penguin, 2014.

Susskind, Lawrence, and Hallam Movius. *Built to Win: Creating a World-Class Negotiating Organization.* Boston: Harvard Business Press, 2009.

Swart, Tara, Kitty Chisholm, and Paul Brown. *Neuroscience for Leadership.* London: Palgrave, 2015.

Toffler, Alvin. *Future Shock.* New York: Bantam Books, 1970.

Twenge, Jean M., and W. Keith Campbell. *The Narcissism Epidemic: Living in the Age of Entitlement.* New York: Free Press, 2009.

Index